Blackstone's Police Manual

Road Policing

Blackstone's Police Manual

Volume 3

Road Policing

2020

John Watson

BSc (Hons), LLB (Hons), PGCE

OXFORD
UNIVERSITY PRESS

OXFORD
UNIVERSITY PRESS

Great Clarendon Street, Oxford, OX2 6DP,
United Kingdom

Oxford University Press is a department of the University of Oxford.
It furthers the University's objective of excellence in research, scholarship,
and education by publishing worldwide. Oxford is a registered trade mark of
Oxford University Press in the UK and in certain other countries

© Oxford University Press, 2019

The moral rights of the author have been asserted

First Edition published in 1998
Twenty-second Edition published in 2019

Impression: 1

Published in the United States of America by Oxford University Press
198 Madison Avenue, New York, NY 10016, United States of America

British Library Cataloguing in Publication Data

Data available

ISBN 978–0–19–884826–4

Printed in Great Britain by
Bell & Bain Ltd., Glasgow

Foreword for 2020 Blackstone's Police Manuals

The police service currently faces a series of challenges, from the changes that police forces must make to deliver savings and reduce crime, to the increasing complexity of the threats to national security, public safety and public order. Underpinning the ability of officers to deal effectively with these challenges are the knowledge and understanding of relevant law and procedure, and the skills to apply this on a daily basis. This understanding is the cornerstone in providing a professional policing service.

The College of Policing plays a vital role in the development of police officers and staff, helping them to obtain and retain the skills and knowledge they need to fight crime and protect the public. The College has a remit to develop, maintain and test standards to ensure suitability for promotion. Part of this responsibility requires the College to ensure a comprehensive and relevant syllabus is produced. As such, the College works alongside Oxford University Press to ensure these Manuals are an accurate and up-to-date source of information and that they reflect what is required by people working across policing.

The *Blackstone's Police Manuals 2020* are the definitive reference source and official study guide for the national legal examination which all candidates must successfully pass in order to be promoted to sergeant or inspector. Their content is derived from evidence gathered from operational sergeants and inspectors alongside input from the wider police service. Whilst they are primarily designed to support officers seeking to progress their careers in preparing for their promotion examinations, they also provide a reference point for officers and staff seeking to continue their professional development and maintain their knowledge as a professional in policing. If you are using these Manuals to prepare for your promotion examinations I would like to take this opportunity to wish you the very best of luck in your studies, and I hope these books will assist you in progressing your career within the police service.

Mike Cunningham
Chief Executive Officer
of the College of Policing

Preface

Road policing covers many areas of community life and brings the police into contact with a significant percentage of the population. Those tasked with road policing are given a whole array of practical powers, from inspecting documentation and checking registration details to stopping and redirecting traffic and removing vehicles. These features present the police with valuable opportunities to pursue immediate priorities associated with traffic policing (such as safety and traffic management) and to disrupt the activities of serious and organised criminals and terrorists. Although much of the activity is high profile, information obtained from road policing is capable of providing invaluable criminal intelligence within the National Intelligence Model. Add to this the considerable numbers of people killed or injured on the roads each year, together with the impact of dangerous, aggressive or simply anti-social driving on the quality of life in the community, and road policing acquires a very important role.

The *Blackstone's Police Manuals* are the only official study guides for Police Promotion Examinations—if the law is not in the Manuals, it will not be in the exams.

All the Manuals include explanatory keynotes and case law examples, providing clear and incisive analysis of important areas. As well as covering basic law and procedure they take full account of the PACE Codes of Practice and human rights implications. They can also be used as a training resource for student police officers, special constables and PCSOs or as an invaluable reference tool for police staff of all ranks and positions.

Oxford University Press are always happy to receive any useful written feedback from any reader on the content and style of the Manual, especially from those involved in or with the criminal justice system. Please email this address with any comments or queries: police.uk@oup.com.

The law is stated as at 1 June 2019.

Acknowledgements

I would like to thank the many people who assisted in the production of this year's Manual. Particular thanks go to the staff at the College of Policing.

Also, thanks to the production, editorial and marketing team at OUP, especially Peter Daniell and Amy Baker.

John Watson

Contents

Table of Cases

Table of Statutes

Table of Statutory Instruments

Table of European Legislation

Table of International Treaties and Conventions

How to use this Manual

Volume numbers for the Manuals

The 2020 Blackstone's Police Manuals each have a volume number as follows:

Volume 1: *Crime*
Volume 2: *Evidence and Procedure*
Volume 3: *Road Policing*
Volume 4: *General Police Duties*

The first digit of each paragraph number in the text of the Manuals denotes the Manual number. For example, chapter 2.3 is chapter 3 of the *Evidence and Procedure* Manual and chapter 4.3 is chapter 3 of the *General Police Duties* Manual.

All index entries and references in the Tables of Legislation and the Table of Cases, etc. refer to paragraph numbers instead of page numbers, making information easier to find.

Material outside the scope of the police promotion examinations syllabus—blacklining

These Manuals contain some information which is outside the scope of the police promotion examinations. A full black line down the margin indicates that the text beside it is excluded from Inspectors' examinations.

PACE Code Chapters

The PACE Codes of Practice have been taken out of the appendices and are now incorporated within chapters in the main body of the Blackstone's Police Manuals. A thick grey line down the margin is used to denote text that is an extract of the PACE Code itself (i.e. the actual wording of the legislation) and does not form part of the general commentary of the chapter.

The PACE Codes of Practice form an important part of the police promotion examinations syllabus and are examinable for both Sergeants and Inspectors. They are not to be confused with 'blacklined' content that is excluded from the syllabus for Inspectors' examinations (see 'Material outside the scope of the police promotion examinations syllabus—blacklining' section).

Length of sentence for an offence

Where a length of sentence for an offence is stated in this Manual, please note that the number of months or years stated is the maximum number and will not be exceeded.

Any feedback regarding content or other editorial matters in the Manuals can be emailed to police.uk@oup.com.

Police Promotion Examinations Rules and Syllabus Information

The rules and syllabus for the police promotion examinations system are defined within the Rules & Syllabus document published by College of Policing Selection and Assessment on behalf of the Police Promotion Examinations Board (PPEB). The Rules & Syllabus document is published annually each September, and applies to all police promotion assessments scheduled for the calendar year following its publication. For example, the September 2019 Rules & Syllabus document would apply to all police promotion assessments held during 2020.

The document provides details of the law and procedure to be tested within the National Police Promotion Framework Step 2 Legal Examination, and also outlines the rules underpinning the police promotion examination system.

All candidates who are taking a police promotion examination are strongly encouraged to familiarise themselves with the Rules & Syllabus document during their preparation. The police promotion examination rules apply to candidates undertaking the National Police Promotion Framework.

The document can be downloaded from the Development Section of the College of Policing website, which can be found at <https://www.college.police.uk>. Electronic versions are also supplied to all force examination officers.

If you have any problems obtaining the Rules & Syllabus document from the above source, please contact the Candidate Administration Team via the 'Contact us' section of the College of Policing website (see above).

Usually, no further updates to the Rules & Syllabus document will be issued during its year-long lifespan. However, in exceptional circumstances, the College of Policing (on behalf of the PPEB) reserves the right to issue an amended syllabus prior to the next scheduled annual publication date.

For example, a major change to a key area of legislation or procedure (e.g. the Codes of Practice) during the lifespan of the current Rules & Syllabus document would render a significant part of the current syllabus content obsolete. In such circumstances, it may be necessary for an update to the syllabus to be issued, which would provide guidance to candidates on any additional material which would be examinable within their police promotion examinations.

In such circumstances, an update to the Rules & Syllabus document would be made available through the College of Policing website, and would be distributed to all force examination contacts. The College of Policing will ensure that any syllabus update is distributed well in advance of the examination date, to ensure that candidates have sufficient time to familiarise themselves with any additional examinable material. Where possible, any additional study materials would be provided to candidates free of charge.

Please note that syllabus updates will only be made in *exceptional* circumstances; an update will not be made for every change to legislation included within the syllabus. For further guidance on this issue, candidates are advised to check regularly the College of Policing website, or consult their force examination officer, during their preparation period.

3.1 Definitions and Principles

3.1.1 Introduction

The key to any offence or power in law is the wording; this leads to the 'points to prove'. Throughout road policing legislation there are a number of key definitions like 'motor vehicle', 'mechanically propelled vehicle' etc. It is fundamental to understanding the points to prove that you understand these definitions and, therefore, it is the key starting point to this Manual.

3.1.2 Key Definitions

The most commonly used road traffic definitions such as 'motor vehicle', 'driver' and 'road' can be found in ss. 185 and 192 of the Road Traffic Act 1988. It is these and other frequently encountered definitions that this chapter deals with.

Sections 185 and 192 provide further definitions whose use is less frequent—where this is the case the relevant definition is given and explained within the chapter dealing with that area of road policing law. This is also the case where legislation other than the Road Traffic Act 1988 provides a specific definition.

3.1.3 Vehicle

A 'vehicle' is not, of itself, defined in the Road Traffic Act 1988. The *Oxford English Dictionary* defines 'vehicle' as a 'carriage or conveyance of any kind used on land'. Virtually anything may be capable of amounting to a 'vehicle' under the right circumstances, even a chicken shed on wheels (*Garner* v *Burr* [1951] 1 KB 31) or a hut used as an office and being drawn along by a tractor (*Horn* v *Dobson* [1933] JC 1). In some circumstances a pram may be a vehicle as may a scooter. A good example of a vehicle is a bicycle.

3.1.4 Mechanically Propelled Vehicle

The term 'mechanically propelled vehicle' is not defined in the Road Traffic Acts. It is ultimately a matter of fact and degree for the court to decide. At its most basic level it is a vehicle which can be propelled by mechanical means. It can include electrical vehicles.

Case law decisions provide us with greater insight as to what this phrase actually means:

• The test as to whether a vehicle is 'mechanically propelled' is one of construction rather than use (*McEachran* v *Hurst* [1978] RTR 462). In this case the defendant was pedalling a moped to a friend's house for repair. It was not taxed and there was no current test certificate in force for the moped. The justices held that it was not a mechanically propelled vehicle on the grounds that it was being used as a pedal cycle, the engine did not work and there was no petrol in the tank. The Divisional Court, reversing the justices' decision, held that the test to be applied to determine whether the moped was mechanically propelled was the same as any other motor vehicle, namely, *on its construction*. If it was constructed as a motor vehicle, it remained a mechanically propelled vehicle unless it could be said that there was no reasonable prospect of it again being mechanically propelled.

- The test will be an objective one which looks at what the vehicle was constructed to do; it does not look at the subjective intention of the owner (*Chief Constable of Avon and Somerset* v *Fleming* [1987] 1 All ER 318).
- The term 'mechanically propelled' not only includes petrol-driven and oil-driven vehicles, but also includes steam and electrically powered vehicles (*Elieson* v *Parker* (1917) 81 JP 265).
- A vehicle which has more than one source of power does not cease to be 'mechanically propelled', even though it is propelled by means other than an engine at the relevant time (*Floyd* v *Bush* [1953] 1 WLR 242).
- In *Newbury* v *Simmonds* [1961] 2 QB 354 it was held that a motor car from which the engine had been removed did not thereby cease to be a mechanically propelled vehicle if the evidence admitted the possibility that the engine might shortly be replaced and the motive power restored. It might be different if the motive power were permanently removed.
- The prosecution bears the burden of showing that a vehicle meets the requirements of being 'mechanically propelled' (*Reader* v *Bunyard* [1987] RTR 406).

3.1.5 Motor Vehicle

The term 'motor vehicle' is defined in s. 185(1) of the Road Traffic Act 1988 and s. 136(1) of the Road Traffic Regulation Act 1984 as 'a mechanically propelled vehicle (**see para. 3.1.4**), intended or adapted for use on roads'. The word 'adapted' means 'altered so as to make it fit' (*Maddox* v *Storer* [1963] 1 QB 451).

Although this is the legal definition, ultimately it is a matter of fact and degree for a court to interpret whether or not a vehicle is a motor vehicle.

The objective approach in deciding whether a vehicle is 'mechanically propelled' is also applied when deciding whether a vehicle is a 'motor vehicle', i.e. the test as to whether a vehicle is intended or adapted for use on roads is an objective one—would a reasonable person say that one of its uses would be general use on a road (*Burns* v *Currell* [1963] 2 QB 433)? It has nothing to do with the owner's or manufacturer's intention. An example of this approach can be seen in *Nichol* v *Leach* [1972] RTR 476, where the owner of a Mini car rebuilt it solely for 'auto-cross' racing, never intending it to be used on a road. Nevertheless, it was held to have retained its original intended road use character and remained a 'motor vehicle'.

Several cases involving 'personal transport' are worthy of note. In *Chief Constable of North Yorkshire Police* v *Saddington* [2001] RTR 15 a 'Go-Ped' (a motorised scooter) was sold with the specific instruction from the manufacturer that it was not to be used on a road. The Divisional Court emphasised the fact that the test was whether a reasonable person would say that one of its uses would be on the road. The court decided that the design and capabilities of the 'Go-Ped', allied with the fact that it offered an opportunity to get quickly through traffic, meant that general use on the road had to be contemplated. The distributor's advice would, in practice, be ignored and its use on a road would not be an isolated occurrence—it was therefore a 'motor vehicle'.

In *DPP* v *King* [2008] EWHC 447 (Admin) the defendant was stopped by the police while riding a 'City Mantis' electric scooter on a public road. The scooter looked like a bicycle except that it did not have any pedals or other means of manual propulsion and it was capable of speeds up to 10 miles per hour. The defendant was charged with driving a motor vehicle while disqualified and with no insurance. At trial, the issue arose regarding whether the scooter was a motor vehicle. The defendant was acquitted, but following the case being passed to the High Court it was remitted with a direction to convict as the court decided that the scooter was a motor vehicle according to s. 185(1) of the Road Traffic Act 1988.

The Segway Personal Transporter is powered by electricity and transports a passenger, standing on a platform propelled on two or more wheels, at speeds up to 12 miles per hour. In *Coates* v *CPS* (2011) EWHC 2032 (Admin) it was decided that the Segway was a 'motor vehicle' as the court pointed out that it took no stretch of the imagination to contemplate that any user of the Segway on a pavement would be tempted to ride on the road when convenient.

'Self-balancing scooters' or 'personal transportation devices' (hover boards) are illegal to ride on the road, because they do not meet the requirements to be registered under either the European or British schemes for road-legal vehicles and it is an offence under s. 72 of the Highway Act 1835 to ride on a pavement.

Note that a motor vehicle continues to be such if it is towed by another vehicle (*Cobb* v *Whorton* [1971] RTR 392).

A diesel dumper truck used solely for road construction work and not intended to be driven along the parts of the highway open to the public has been held *not* to be a motor vehicle for insurance purposes (*MacDonald* v *Carmichael* 1941 JC 27). Dumper trucks intended for use solely on construction sites will not be 'motor vehicles' but, if you are able to adduce evidence that they *are suitable* for use on a road, they may be held to be motor vehicles (*Daley* v *Hargreaves* [1961] 1 WLR 487). They will, of course, still be 'mechanically propelled vehicles' even when used elsewhere than on a road.

Section 189 of the Road Traffic Act 1988 specifies which vehicles will *not* be treated as motor vehicles; they include pedestrian controlled vehicles, some implements for cutting grass and electrically assisted pedal cycles.

3.1.6 Driver

Section 192(1) of the Road Traffic Act 1988 states that the 'driver' is a 'person engaged in the driving of the vehicle'.

It is possible for more than one person to be the 'driver' of a vehicle. In *Tyler* v *Whatmore* [1976] RTR 83 it was held that a girl in the front passenger seat of a car who leaned across the person in the driver's seat with both of her hands on the steering wheel, steering the car, with the ignition switch and handbrake within her reach, was 'actually driving'. Her companion in the driving seat whose view she obstructed and who was controlling the propulsion of the car but could not control the steering was also driving.

Whether a person supervising a driver from the passenger's seat is a driver will be defined by the degree of control exercised throughout by the supervisor. An instructor who retains simultaneous control of the car by keeping hands on the brake and steering wheel may be the driver (*Langman* v *Valentine* [1952] 2 All ER 803), however where the instructor was only in a position to assume control if necessary and therefore not in control at the material time he was held not to be the 'driver' (*Evans* v *Walkden* [1956] 1 WLR 1019). These cases, of course, pre-date dual control learner vehicles but would relate to non-dual control vehicles.

For the purposes of some road traffic offences, the person who takes out the vehicle remains the 'driver' of it until that journey ends. Therefore, even if the vehicle is stationary and has been for some time, a person may still be the 'driver' of it if the journey has not ended (see *Jones* v *Prothero* [1952] 1 All ER 434 where the driver sitting in a parked car opened the offside door causing injury to a passing pedal cyclist). Another example is *Cawthorn (Jonathan)* v *DPP* [2000] RTR 45 where the defendant stopped his car on a hill to post a letter and activated the hazard warning lights. While he was away from the vehicle, it rolled down the hill and hit a wall that was damaged (the roll was started by a passenger releasing the handbrake). The defendant left the scene and was subsequently convicted of failing to stop and exchange details and failing to report an accident. The Divisional Court said that, although there had been a break in the driving, the appellant was still making his journey (evidenced by the use of the hazard warning lights). The intervening act by the passenger did not make that passenger the driver. Both *Jones* and *Cawthorn* related to the obligations of a 'driver' under s. 170 of the Road Traffic Act 1988 (**see chapter 3.4**).

Whether a person was actually the driver of a vehicle at a particular time *cannot be inferred* from the fact that he/she is also the owner; more evidence of his/her actual involvement in the driving of the vehicle will be required (*R v Collins* [1994] RTR 216) and all evidence, including circumstantial evidence, can be considered (*McCombie v CPS* [2011] EWHC 758 (Admin)).

The term 'driver' also includes a separate person acting as a steersman of a motor vehicle under s. 192(1) of the 1988 Act (except for the purposes of an offence of causing death by dangerous driving under s. 1 of the 1988 Act (**see para. 3.3.2**)).

3.1.7 Drive and Driving

The Road Traffic Act 1988 does not define 'drive' but directs that 'drive' is to be interpreted according to the definition of 'driver' in s. 192(1) which simply refers to a person using the driver's controls for the purpose of directing the movement of the vehicle. This phrase has been enhanced by the decisions of the courts so that there are a number of different situations where a person can be said to be 'driving' a vehicle (even though they do not conjure up a picture of conventional driving).

The leading case is *R v MacDonagh* [1974] RTR 372. The circumstances related to whether a person who pushed a car along a road with both feet on the ground with one arm in the car to control the steering wheel could be said to be 'driving'—it was held that this *was not* driving (the behaviour was described as 'pushing'). This decision provides several determining factors to be considered when deciding if a person is 'driving':

- Whether a person is 'driving' or not is a question of fact, dependent on the degree and extent to which the person has control of the direction and movement of the vehicle.
- If the person is in control of the direction and movement of the vehicle, is that control 'in a substantial sense'?
- Even if the control of the direction and movement of the vehicle can be said to be 'in a substantial sense', it must still be considered whether the activity in question could fall within the ordinary meaning of the word 'driving' in the English language.

It was suggested (in *MacDonagh*) that it would be possible to find as a fact that a person was driving if a motorist pushing the vehicle had one foot in the car in order to make more effective use of the controls. This may seem like a fine distinction—two feet on the road is 'pushing', one foot on the road and the other in the car is potentially 'driving'—but then there must come a tipping point where 'driving' behaviour begins or ends and wherever that may be it is likely to be the slightest of actions that alters the balance one way or the other.

Later case law decisions have established additional tests to *MacDonagh*:

- Did the defendant deliberately set the vehicle in motion? In *Burgoyne v Phillips* [1983] RTR 49, the defendant was sitting behind the steering wheel of a car. Assuming he still had the keys in the ignition, he let the car roll forward to drive off carefully. He realised he had no keys in the ignition and put the brakes on quickly. The steering wheel was locked and the engine was not running. The car rolled a distance of 30ft by gravity and collided with another vehicle. The defendant was held to be 'driving'.

- How long did the defendant have control of the direction and movement of the vehicle? In *Jones* v *Pratt* [1983] RTR 54, the Divisional Court held that the front seat passenger in a moving car who momentarily grabbed the steering wheel, pushing it in a clockwise direction, causing the car to leave the road (behaviour carried out to prevent an accident), could not properly be described as 'driving' in the ordinary sense of the word.

It is also worth examining verdicts dealing with more specific circumstances.

Driving

- In *DPP* v *Alderton* [2003] EWHC 2917 (Admin) it was held that operating the controls of a car (accelerator, clutch and steering) which was parked on a grass verge and wheel spinning was 'driving' even though there was no movement of the vehicle.
- A person may be 'driving' even though he/she is only attempting to control the movement of the vehicle. In *Rowan* v *Merseyside Chief Constable* (1985), *The Times*, 10 December, the defendant knelt on the driving seat, released the handbrake and thereafter attempted to re-apply it to stop the movement of the vehicle—he was held to be 'driving'.
- A steersman in a motor vehicle towed by a rope or chain can properly be said to be 'driving'. In *McQuaid* v *Anderton* [1981] 1 WLR 154 the defendant sat in the driver's seat of a motor car while it was being towed by means of a tow rope connected to another vehicle. He steered the towed car and was able to use its brakes as and when required.
- In *Gunnel* v *DPP* [1994] RTR 151 the appellant was convicted of driving a motor vehicle, a moped, with excess alcohol. When he had attempted to start it, the engine did not fire, and he set the moped in motion by sitting astride it and propelling it with his feet in a 'paddling' movement—this was held to be 'driving'. If he were not sitting astride it but pushing it while walking alongside it then he would not have been 'driving' (*MacDonagh*).

Not Driving

- The Divisional Court has accepted a finding that a person sitting in the driver's seat of a car with the *engine running* had been 'driving' (*R (On the Application of Planton)* v *DPP* [2001] EWHC 450 (Admin)). This was extended in *Mason* v *DPP* [2010] RTR 120 where the Divisional Court suggested that 'driving' would occur when turning on the engine. This can be compared to the situation where the person sitting in the driving seat of a stationary motor vehicle with hands on the steering wheel and the *engine off*, was held *not* to be 'driving' (*Leach* v *DPP* [1993] RTR 161).
- In *Blayney* v *Knight* [1975] RTR 279, a taxi driver left his taxi, which had automatic transmission, with the engine running. The defendant, who had no intention of driving, sat in the driver's seat. In the course of a struggle with the taxi driver, the defendant's foot touched the accelerator causing the taxi to drive along the road, mount a pavement and swerve back to the offside. The defendant was held *not* to be 'driving'.

Once the act of 'driving' has commenced, it continues until it terminates. This may sound obvious but the question for the court is precisely when does it terminate? A person may still be 'driving' although the vehicle is stationary, when he/she is buying a newspaper or changing a wheel (*Pinner* v *Everett* [1969] 1 WLR 1266; also consider *Cawthorn (Jonathan)* v *DPP* [2000] RTR 45 at **para. 3.1.6**). In *Edkins* v *Knowles* [1973] QB 748, it was emphasised that the reason for stopping is relevant, as it might be part of the journey, e.g. stopping at a set of traffic lights or a junction, or may mark a break in the journey, in which case the length of the break and whether the driver leaves the vehicle is important. The court must consider the period of time and the circumstances to decide whether the person still in the driver's seat (or not as the case may be) was 'driving'.

There must be admissible *evidence* of the features relating to 'driving'. Mere *suspicion* on the part of the arresting or reporting officer will not be sufficient to prove this aspect of the relevant offence (*R (On the Application of Huntley)* v *DPP* [2004] EWHC 870 (Admin)).

3.1.8 Attempting to Drive

The Criminal Attempts Act 1981 (s. 1) states that if a person does an act which is *more than merely preparatory* to the commission of an offence, then he/she is guilty of attempting to commit the offence. This approach is taken when deciding if someone is attempting to drive, i.e. is what this person is doing *more than merely preparatory to the act of driving*? Opening the door of a car is clearly preparatory (*Mason* v *DPP* [2010] RTR 120) but whether the person has done something that is more than merely preparatory to driving is a question of fact to be decided on the individual circumstances of the case.

The general approach to attempts under s. 1 of the Criminal Attempts Act 1981 is that one can attempt the impossible. This is also the case when considering whether someone is attempting to drive, so where the defendant was found revving the engine of a motor car which in fact could not be driven because the clutch had burnt out, he was still 'attempting to drive' (*R* v *Farrance* [1978] RTR 225). Likewise, when an unfit driver, who had no ignition key, sat in the driver's seat and attempted to insert other keys into the ignition, he was held to be properly convicted of attempting to drive (*Kelly* v *Hogan* [1982] RTR 352).

3.1.9 In Charge

The principles to be applied when considering whether a person is 'in charge' of a vehicle are set out in *DPP* v *Watkins* [1989] 2 WLR 966. Two different situations might arise:

- Where the defendant is the owner or lawful possessor of the vehicle or where the defendant has recently driven it. In these cases it would be for the defendant to show that he/she was no longer in charge of it and that there was no likelihood of resuming control at the relevant time (e.g. while drunk).
- Where the defendant is not the owner, lawful possessor or has not recently driven the vehicle but was sitting in the vehicle or otherwise involved with it. In these cases the prosecution must show that the defendant was in voluntary control of the vehicle or intended to become so in the immediate future.

The circumstances to be taken into account will vary, but the following would be relevant:

- whether the defendant was in possession of a key that fitted the ignition;
- where the defendant was in relation to the vehicle at the time and what he was doing;
- what evidence there is of the defendant's intention to take or assert control of the vehicle by driving or otherwise.

It is possible to be in charge of a motor vehicle even though it is immobile (*Drake* v *DPP* [1994] RTR 411).

In *DPP* v *Janman* [2004] EWHC 101 (Admin), the defendant was supervising his partner, a provisional licence-holder, who was driving the car. He failed a breath test and was prosecuted for being in charge of the vehicle. He argued that he had no need to supervise the driver as she was able to drive. The Administrative Court concluded that although there might be circumstances in which a supervisor might be able to prove that there was no likelihood of driving, that was likely to be a difficult task. A supervisor was required because provisional licence-holders are not yet deemed competent to drive on their own and a supervisor must be prepared at any time to take over responsibility for the vehicle—the defendant was manifestly 'in charge'.

3.1.10　Road

A road is defined under s. 192(1) of the Road Traffic Act 1988 as:

> …any highway and any other road to which the public has access, and includes bridges over which a road passes.

This definition is applicable to most occasions where the expression 'road' is used in statutes.

Generally a road stretches to the boundary fences adjacent to it, including any pavements and grass verges (*Worth* v *Brooks* [1959] Crim LR 855). In *Price* v *DPP* [1990] RTR 413, where the defendant drove across a pavement (part of which was maintained at public expense and part of which was privately owned) thereby causing a pedestrian to jump out of the way, it was held that the pavement as a whole constituted a road.

A useful description of a 'road' comes from the House of Lords in *Cutter* v *Eagle Star Insurance Co. Ltd* [1997] 1 WLR 1082. While it remained a question of fact in every case, a 'road' had the physical character of a defined or definable route or way, with ascertained or ascertainable edges, leading from one point to another with the function of serving as a means of access enabling travellers to move conveniently from one point to another along that route. The function of a car park was to enable stationary vehicles to stand and wait. In the ordinary use of language a car park was not a road; they have separate and distinct characters. Where legislation referred to 'a road or other public place', the express addition of the words 'or other public place' clearly indicates that, where the word 'road' stands alone, it bears its ordinary meaning and does not extend to places such as car parks. In the event of a carriageway being found to exist within its bounds which does so qualify, the remaining area will retain its integrity as a car park (*Clarke* v *Kato* [1998] 1 WLR 1647).

A 'highway' is a way over which the public has a right to pass and re-pass by foot, horse or vehicle, or with animals (*Lang* v *Hindhaugh* [1986] RTR 271). For a highway to exist, there must be some form of 'dedication' of the relevant land to the public and, once so dedicated, it is unlikely that the public status of a highway can be changed. A highway does not cease to be such when it is temporarily roped off or closed (*McCrone* v *J and L Rigby (Wigan) Ltd* (1950) 50 LGR 115). Highways include public bridleways and footpaths; and include public bridges over which they pass. Bridleways are highways where the public have a right to ride or lead horses (and related animals) or to pass on foot.

Whether the public has access is a question of fact and degree (*R* v *Waterfield* [1964] 1 QB 164). In *Harrison* v *Hill* 1932 JC 13, a road leading off the public road to a farmhouse was held to be a road to which the public had access. The road had no gate and was maintained by the farmer, who sometimes turned away people using it, but at all other times it was used by people with no business at the farm at all.

In any case where use by the public may not be readily apparent, *Hallett* v *DPP* [2011] EWHC 488 (Admin) emphasises the need for the prosecution to adduce evidence of such. If only a restricted section of the public (such as members of a club) has access to a road, that is not enough to make it a 'road' (*Blackmore* v *Chief Constable of Devon and Cornwall* (1984) *The Times*, 6 December). Any access enjoyed by the public must be with the agreement of the landowner. So members of the public must not have obtained access 'either by overcoming a physical obstruction or in defiance of prohibition, express or implied'. Therefore roads are capable of being closed or cordoned off in a way that alters their status as such.

If a vehicle is partly on a road and partly on some other privately owned land it can be treated as being 'on a road' for the purposes of road traffic legislation (*Randall* v *Motor Insurers' Bureau* [1968] 1 WLR 1900). A car supported by roller skates so that its wheels did not touch the surface of a road was held to be 'on a road' even though it was not in actual physical contact with the road (*Holliday* v *Henry* [1974] RTR 101). In *Avery* v *CPS* [2012] RTR 87, where the physical boundary of the road was in issue, it being asserted that the wheels of the vehicle driven by the defendant remained on a private driveway, the

Divisional Court held that any material encroachment on the air-space vertically above the road was sufficient to justify a conclusion that the vehicle concerned was 'on a road'.

3.1.11 Public Place

In order to prove that a place is in fact a 'public place' for the purposes of road traffic offences, it must be shown by the prosecution that:

- those people who are admitted to the place in question are members of the public and are admitted as such, not as members of some special or particular class of the public (e.g. people belonging to an exclusive club) or as a result of some special characteristic that is not shared by the public at large (e.g. those delivering goods or meter readers); *and*
- people are so admitted with the permission, express or implied, of the owner of the land in question.

(*DPP* v *Vivier* [1991] RTR 205)

Whether a place is a 'public place' will be a question of fact for the court. Some examples of places which have been held to qualify as 'public places' are:

- a privately owned caravan site open to campers (*Vivier*);
- a school playground used outside school hours as a leisure park by members of the public (*Rodger* v *Normand* 1995 SLT 411);
- a field used in connection with an agricultural show (*Paterson* v *Ogilvy* 1957 SLT 354);
- a multi-storey car park (*Bowman* v *DPP* [1991] RTR 263);
- a car park attached to commercial premises intended only for the use of customers but accessible *from* a public place and with no restrictions placed on people entering the car park (*May* v *DPP* [2005] EWHC 1280 (Admin)).

For a place which is ostensibly *public* in its nature to become a *private* place, either permanently or temporarily, there needs to be some form of physical obstruction to be overcome in order to enter that place (*R* v *Waters* (1963) 47 Cr App R 149). Therefore a pub landlord, by ordering people to leave the car park of his pub, had not done enough to turn what was a public place (the car park during opening hours) into a private place.

In deciding whether or not a place is in fact a 'public place', magistrates may use their own local knowledge, but must be circumspect in doing so (*Clift* v *Long* [1961] Crim LR 121).

Police officers must provide enough evidence to show that a particular location is a public place. In *R* v *DPP, ex parte Taussik* [2001] ACD 10 the defendant was stopped as she drove out of an access road leading from a block of flats. The access road was a cul-de-sac leading off a highway and was maintained by the local housing department. At the entrance to it there was a large sign saying 'Private Residents Only'. Following her conviction under s. 5(1)(b) of the Road Traffic Act 1988, the defendant appealed, alleging that the sign on the access road excluded anyone other than residents from using it and therefore it was not a 'public place'. The Divisional Court took the view that the evidence of the police officers as to the actual use of the access road by other people was very thin. As there was no evidence from the officers themselves that they had seen motorists (other than residents) using the road, the court was unable to conclude that the road was anything other than a private one. The court held that, as the issue of whether a place is a 'public place' or not is largely a question of fact, it is essential that the prosecution present clear evidence showing who uses the road, when and for what purpose.

However, in a case involving a motorist stopped in a pub car park, the police witness did not adduce specific evidence that the car park was in fact a public place at the time of the offence. Nevertheless, the Divisional Court went on to hold that it was clear from previous authorities that a car park was certainly *capable* of being a public place and this was more likely when its use was not restricted to a particular group of people. Therefore it could properly be inferred that the car park, attached as it was to a pub to which members of the public were generally invited by the landlord, was in fact a public place. The court held that it was not necessary for the prosecution to adduce evidence to show that the car park was a public place and that the magistrates were entitled to reach the decision that they had (*R (On the Application of Lewis)* v *DPP* [2004] EWHC 3081 (Admin)).

3.1.12   Use, Cause or Permit

The concepts of using, causing or permitting are central to many road policing offences. If there is any doubt as to which offence is appropriate it is acceptable to charge 'using' *or* 'causing' *or* 'permitting' as alternatives (*Ross Hillman Ltd* v *Bond* [1974] QB 435) but the advice of the local CPS should be sought.

3.1.12.1   Use

The term 'using' within the context of use, cause or permit has a restrictive meaning and must involve an element of controlling, managing or operating the vehicle by the person concerned (*Hatton* v *Hall* [1997] RTR 212).

The 'using' of a vehicle is generally, though not exclusively, restricted to:

- the driver;
- the driver's employer (when the driver is driving the vehicle on the employer's business).

In *West Yorkshire Trading Standards* v *Lex Vehicle Leasing Ltd* [1996] RTR 70, the Court of Appeal restricted the meaning of the word 'use' when it appears alongside 'cause' and 'permit'. In such circumstances 'using' is restricted to the driver or owner of the vehicle and, in the case of the owner, only if he/she employed the driver under a contract of service and at the material time the vehicle was being driven on the owner's business.

Where the expression 'use' does not appear alongside 'cause' and 'permit' the concept is wider.

If a person driving a vehicle is doing so in the ordinary course of the employer's business, the employer is *using* the vehicle. In such a case you must prove that:

- the defendant (employer) actually owned the vehicle;
- at the relevant time, the driver was employed by the defendant; and
- the driver was driving the vehicle in the ordinary course of his/her employment.

(*Jones* v *DPP* [1999] RTR 1)

It is immaterial that the employer has not specifically authorised the employee to use the vehicle in such a way (*Richardson* v *Baker* [1976] RTR 56).

If the driver is not an employee then the employer is not using the vehicle, even if that driver is a partner of the firm or has been asked to drive the vehicle by the employer (*Crawford* v *Haughton* [1972] 1 WLR 572). The employer may, however, be shown to be 'causing' or 'permitting'.

If a garage lends one of its vehicles to a customer and the customer then uses the vehicle on his/her own business, the garage cannot be said to be 'using' the vehicle (*Dove (LF)* v *Tarvin* (1964) 108 SJ 404).

If a vehicle is shown to be a 'motor vehicle' and on a 'road', it may be said to be in 'use' even if it is in such a state that it cannot be driven (*Pumbien* v *Vines* [1996] RTR 37). There is no need to show some element of control or operation of the vehicle by the owner in order to prove 'use'.

Vehicles left unattended on a road can still be regarded as being used, as 'use' has been held to mean 'having some use of' for these purposes (*Eden* v *Mitchell* [1975] RTR 425).

Accordingly, the mere fact of having two defective tyres did not preclude the vehicle's use and the owner's intention in relation to the vehicle was held to be irrelevant. Therefore, if a vehicle is not in a roadworthy condition it can still be available for the owner's use even though the owner has no intention of utilising it while it remains in that state.

It should be noted that the Divisional Court has applied a broader interpretation to the meaning of 'use' when considering offences involving *trailers*. The court held that the owner of a defective trailer who is responsible for putting it on a road should not be able to escape liability for its condition simply by arguing that it was being drawn and therefore 'used' by someone else (*NFC Forwarding Ltd* v *DPP* [1989] RTR 239).

3.1.12.2 Cause

'Causing' will involve some degree of 'control' or 'dominance' by, or some express mandate from, the *causer*.

Causing requires both positive action and knowledge by the defendant (*Price* v *Cromack* [1975] 1 WLR 988). If the owner of a vehicle is to be shown to have 'caused' an offence to be committed, he/she must be shown to have done something to contribute to it (e.g. by instructing another to drive it) *and also* to have known of any relevant facts (e.g. that it was overloaded) (*Ross Hillman Ltd* v *Bond* [1974] QB 435).

In cases involving employers' vehicles it may be easier to prove 'use' of the vehicle (**see para. 3.1.12.1**).

Wilful blindness by employers to their employees' unlawful actions (e.g. not completing drivers' records) is not enough to amount to 'causing' the offence (*Redhead Freight Ltd* v *Shulman* [1989] RTR 1).

3.1.12.3 Permit

Permitting is less direct or explicit than causing. Permitting involves giving leave or licence to do something (*Houston* v *Buchanan* [1940] 2 All ER 179). The relevant permission (e.g. to use a vehicle in a certain way or subject to some proviso) can be express or it can be inferred by the relevant person (such as where someone is given the use of a friend's car without any conditions being stipulated by the friend).

Generally, in order to prove an offence of 'permitting', you will need to show knowledge by the defendant of the vehicle's *use*, and the *unlawful nature* of that use. However, it is necessary to consider the relevant piece of legislation in each case, together with its intended purpose.

You cannot 'permit' yourself to do something (*Keene* v *Muncaster* [1980] RTR 377).

3.1.13 Defences in Relation to Road Policing Offences

3.1.13.1 Duress and Duress of Circumstances

The defence of duress applies where the defendant has been compelled to commit an offence having been threatened with death or serious physical injury, and duress of circumstances is where circumstances leave the defendant no real alternative but to commit an offence. Whatever the particular arguments for and against the defences, it is clear that they will generally apply to cases of dangerous, careless and inconsiderate driving (they also apply to the offences of driving while disqualified: *R* v *Martin* [1989] RTR 63 and confirmed in *R* v *Backshall* [1998] 1 WLR 1506).

Cases relating to these defences include where the driver was forced to commit the offence in order to avoid death or serious injury (*R* v *Conway* [1989] RTR 35). In *DPP* v *Bell* [1992] RTR 335, the defence was upheld where the defendant needed to drive a vehicle in order to escape serious physical harm, even though he had drunk a considerable amount of alcohol.

However, where the defendant had driven a far greater distance than was necessary to escape the relevant danger, the Divisional Court was not prepared to accept the defence in answer to a charge of driving while over the prescribed limit (*DPP* v *Tomkinson* [2001] EWHC Admin 182).

In *DPP* v *Hicks* [2002] EWHC 1638 (Admin), a case arising out of driving while over the prescribed limit, the Administrative Court set out the following guidelines to be applied before the defences will generally be available to drivers:

- the defence is only available if the driving was undertaken to avoid consequences that could not otherwise have been avoided;
- those consequences must have both been inevitable and involved the risk of serious harm to the driver or someone else for whom the driver was responsible;
- the driver must do no more than is reasonably necessary to avoid the harm;
- the danger of so driving must not be disproportionate to the harm threatened.

However it is clear from *DPP* v *Harris* [1995] RTR 100 (**see para. 3.1.13.3**), that the defence is not available to police officers driving through red traffic lights in an emergency situation.

3.1.13.2 Automatism

Where a person's movements are beyond his/her control or his/her actions are brought about involuntarily, he/she will not generally be liable at criminal law as the element of *actus reus* is not present.

A notable example of this is *automatism*. Where the defendant is deprived of the ability to control his/her movements, he/she may claim that the resulting consequences (e.g. the car swerving or colliding with something) were beyond his/her control and that the defence of automatism should apply. When this happens to the driver of a vehicle, it may remove his/her liability for certain offences such as careless driving. This is because there is no willed action or omission by the defendant. It is also highly unlikely that the defendant would have the required state of mind. Such a situation might be brought about by a swarm of bees flying in through the open window of a moving car or the driver lapsing into a coma (*Hill* v *Baxter* [1958] 1 QB 277).

There must, however, be a 'total destruction of voluntary control'; impaired or reduced control is not enough (*Attorney General's Reference (No. 2 of 1992)* [1994] QB 91). The prosecution must establish the manner of the defendant's driving and then the defendant must adduce evidence that he/she was totally unable to control the car (*C* [2007] EWCA Crim 1862).

If a defendant is suffering from a particular medical condition or is prone to effects which are likely to impair driving ability (such as dizziness—*R* v *Sibbles* [1959] Crim LR 660), he/she has a duty to take reasonable steps to avoid driving when the symptoms are likely to arise. If a diabetic continues to drive while experiencing the start of a hypoglycaemic episode, it is unlikely that the defence of automatism would be available to a charge of careless driving; the diabetic should have stopped driving until the episode had passed (*Moses* v *Winder* [1981] RTR 37).

Similarly, where the loss of voluntary movement or control is brought about by self-induced measures (such as taking/failing to take medication or by drinking), automatism is not generally available as a defence (*R* v *Quick* [1973] QB 910).

Driving in a state of reduced awareness brought on by the continuous focusing on a long, featureless road (sometimes called 'motorway hypnosis') is not enough to raise the defence of automatism (*Attorney-General's Reference (No. 2 of 1992)* [1993] RTR 337).

3.1.13.3 Police Drivers

Police drivers will be judged against the same standard of care as other drivers (*Wood* v *Richards* [1977] RTR 201) and there is no special exemption for them or any other emergency crews (*R v O'Toole* (1971) 55 Cr App R 206). The use of roadside cameras for detecting and prosecuting drivers for exceeding the applicable speed limit and passing through red lights has resulted in a significant increase in the number of emergency services vehicles being reported. As the vast majority of such cases fall within the legal parameters either for speed limits or for passing through lights at red, the government and NPCC (along with others) have signed up to a protocol. Part of the protocol operates by making assumptions that, where the photograph shows flashing lights being displayed on the vehicle, the relevant exemption applied (in the absence of evidence to the contrary). This protocol is of practical effect in reducing the bureaucratic burden on the system of roadside cameras; it does not affect the substantive law which the rest of this paragraph addresses. However, police drivers are granted some exemptions from specific traffic regulation and there are several cases that help in identifying the relevant features that will be applied in determining the driver's liability.

It is also worth bearing in mind that, while the particular circumstances under which the police driver was driving may not provide a specific defence, they may nevertheless provide mitigation and, where appropriate, special reasons for not disqualifying the driver (see e.g. *Agnew v DPP* [1991] RTR 144).

In *R v Bannister* [2009] EWCA Crim 1571, the Court of Appeal ruled that an advanced police driver with highly developed driving skills was *not* entitled to have that ability taken into account when deciding whether or not the driving in question was dangerous. The statutory test is based simply on the standard of the competent and careful driver, who is not to be vested with any particular level of skill or ability not found in the ordinary motorist.

The Court of Appeal's review of the issues of civil liability arising from police drivers (*Keyse v Commissioner of the Metropolitan Police* [2001] EWCA Civ 715) held that:

- Speed alone was not decisive of negligence by a police driver.
- Emergency service vehicles on duty were expressly exempted from the statutory rules for speed limits, keep left signs and traffic lights (s. 87 of the Road Traffic Regulation Act 1984 and regs 15(2) and 33(2) of the Traffic Signs Regulations and General Directions 1994 (SI 1994/1519)) (note the relevant regulation is now reg. 36(1)(b) of the Traffic Signs Regulations and General Directions 2002 (SI 2002/3113)).
- Police and other emergency service drivers were entitled to expect other road users to take note of the signs of their approach (e.g. sirens and flashing lights) and, where appropriate, react accordingly.

Consequently, the court held that a police driver who had accelerated through a green light at a road junction with the vehicle's visual and audible warning equipment in operation was not liable for the injuries to a pedestrian who stepped off the pavement into the path of the vehicle.

Appropriately trained drivers employed by the National Crime Agency will also be covered by emergency drivers' exemptions.

Regulation 33 (now reg. 36(1)(b) of the Traffic Signs Regulations and General Directions 2002) referred to above makes allowances for emergency services drivers to pass through red traffic lights under certain circumstances. The regulations set out the conditions under which a driver may proceed through a red light and failure to meet those conditions will render the driver liable to a charge under s. 2 or 3 of the 1988 Act. Consequently, the driver of a police surveillance vehicle following suspects to the scene of an intended armed robbery could not rely on the fact that he was required by the seriousness of the circumstances to go through a red light when he did so in a way which was not covered by the regulations (*DPP v Harris* [1995] RTR 100). See also *R v Collins* [1997] RTR 439 at **para. 3.3.2.2, Keynote**.

In *Harris*, the Divisional Court held that the wording of the regulation meant that there was no scope for the defence of necessity where police drivers went through red traffic lights. It was held that the exemption for drivers of police vehicles in such circumstances was restricted to the extent that another driver should not be obliged to change speed or course to avoid a collision. The court held that all the driver in *Harris* need have done to avoid the accident was to have stopped for a couple of seconds or to have edged forward slowly.

This view was followed in the civil case of *Griffin* v *Merseyside Regional Ambulance* [1998] PIQR P34, where the Court of Appeal held that the duty of care required of a driver of any emergency vehicle is not to proceed 'in a manner likely to endanger any person' or cause them to change their speed or course of direction (per reg. 33(1)(b), now reg. 36(1)(b) of the Traffic Signs Regulations and General Directions 2002). It is the *manner* of the police officer's driving that must not cause the other driver to be endangered or to change speed or direction. The whole purpose of the audible and visual warning systems on emergency vehicles ('blues and twos') is to alert other drivers and, if necessary, to get them to change speed and/ or direction. Similarly, rule 219 of the Highway Code tells drivers to look and listen for emergency vehicles and to make room for them, pulling over and stopping where necessary provided that does not endanger other road users.

It is perhaps worth noting that, if a person drives in a way which creates a need for police officers to pursue that person and an officer is subsequently injured in that pursuit, that person may owe a duty of care to the police officer and may therefore be sued for damages. In *Langley* v *Dray* [1997] PIQR P508 (confirmed by the Court of Appeal [1998] PIQR P314), the court held that the driver of the stolen motor vehicle owed a duty of care to the police officer pursuing him. He knew or ought to have known that the police were in pursuit and should not have gone so fast on ice. He had a duty not to create such a risk. This decision suggests that there are times when the police can be placed under an obligation by a driver to pursue him/her.

KEYNOTE

The CPS has issued guidance in relation to charging offences arising from driving incidents involving emergency vehicles. These guidelines state:

> In the course of their duties, police officers, ambulance staff and fire-fighters may need to drive a vehicle in response to an emergency in a manner which would otherwise be considered unacceptable. Our starting point is that it is very unlikely to be appropriate to proceed with a prosecution on public interest grounds if a police officer, member of ambulance staff or fire-fighter commits a driving offence while responding to an emergency call.

However, every individual case must be considered on its own facts and merits, and when considering whether it is in the public interest to proceed with the case, prosecutors should have regard to the following factors:

- the nature of the emergency known to or reasonably perceived by the driver, e.g. whether the driver was responding to a 999 call in compliance with the agreed operating practice in that service;
- the level of culpability of the driver (including the nature of the driving); and
- whether there is evidence that the driver may be a continuing danger to others. For example, such evidence may include relevant convictions or internal disciplinary proceedings against the driver.

3.2 | Key Police Powers

3.2.1 Introduction

The Road Traffic Act 1988 provides police officers with numerous powers in respect of road policing matters. This chapter examines several powers that are at the core of many road policing issues—the *essential* power to stop a vehicle (s. 163), the powers to demand documentation and details from the driver (ss. 164 and 165), the associated powers of seizure and retention of vehicles (ss. 165A and 165B) and the duty to give information regarding the identity of the driver (s. 172).

3.2.2 Power to Stop a Vehicle

The Road Traffic Act 1988, s. 163 states:

(1) A person driving a mechanically propelled vehicle on a road must stop the vehicle on being required to do so by a constable in uniform or a traffic officer.
(2) A person riding a cycle on a road must stop the cycle on being required to do so by a constable in uniform or a traffic officer.
(3) If a person fails to comply with this section he is guilty of an offence.

KEYNOTE

The offence of failing to stop is triable summarily and punishable by a fine.

'Stop' has been held to mean bringing the vehicle to a halt and remaining at rest for long enough for the officer to exercise whatever additional powers are appropriate (*Lodwick* v *Saunders* [1985] 1 WLR 382).

Section 163 is a 'Random' Power

The use of s. 163 is not restricted to road traffic matters only—a police officer in uniform may require a person driving a mechanically propelled vehicle on a road to stop it. This is a power for an officer in uniform to *randomly* stop vehicles.

That said, like any power available to the police, its use must be able to be justified. In *Stewart* v *Crowe* 1999 SLT 899, it was said that the power under s. 163 represented a necessary and proportionate response to the prevention of crime and that the only limit on the power is that it should not be used whimsically or oppressively.

Considering the use of the power from the road policing perspective, there may be a wide variety of reasons why a police officer in uniform would stop a vehicle, such as:

- to require the driver to produce his/her driving licence;
- to require the driver to give his/her name and address;
- to require the driver to give the name and address of the owner of the vehicle;
- to require the driver to produce his/her certificate of insurance and/or test certificate;
- to have the vehicle examined to see if it complies with construction and use regulations;
- to have the vehicle examined to see if it is in a dangerous condition.

The courts have accepted that the police are empowered to stop vehicles at random to inquire whether the driver has been drinking. Consider the annual drink/drive campaigns that take place over the Christmas/New Year period—every vehicle passing through such a check-point might be randomly stopped by a police officer in uniform and drivers asked if they have been drinking. The requirement to stop the vehicle is a legal one and as a result of a response given by the driver and/or the officer's observations, a suspicion may form in the officer's mind that the driver has alcohol in his/her body and the officer may require the driver to take a preliminary test. This is a random stop but *not* a random preliminary test (*Miller* v *Bell* 2004 SCCR 534).

In *Chief Constable of Gwent* v *Dash* [1986] RTR 41 vehicles were being randomly stopped in order to give a police officer further experience of the breath test procedure under the supervision of her senior officer. The court held that (what is now) s. 6(2) is concerned only with the provision of breath; it does not bear upon the circumstances in which the driver may be required to stop. The actions of the police were not an abuse of power and did not amount to malpractice; therefore the requirement of a breath specimen and the subsequent procedure were lawful. Random stopping of cars for the purpose of ascertaining whether their drivers have alcohol in their bodies is perfectly permissible; random breath testing, however, is not. This case adds yet another reason for a police officer to stop a vehicle—to train newly appointed officers in traffic procedure.

Constable in Uniform

Whether a constable (which includes an officer of any rank, including special constables) was in uniform at the time is a matter of fact for a court to determine. What counts as 'uniform' is unclear but, if constables can be easily identified from their manner of dress as a police officer, the requirement has probably been met (*Wallwork* v *Giles* [1970] RTR 117; officer without a helmet held to be 'in uniform'). The wearing of an 'ordinary' raincoat over a police uniform (*Taylor* v *Baldwin* [1976] RTR 265) did not affect the conclusion that the officer was still in uniform. Justices are also able to rely on their knowledge of how the local constabulary operates (*Cooper* v *Rowlands* [1971] RTR 291, in relation to a motorway patrol officer, and *Richards* v *West* [1980] RTR 215, in relation to special constables) and, in the absence of evidence to the contrary, they are entitled to infer or assume from the surrounding circumstances that a constable is in uniform (*Gage* v *Jones* [1983] RTR 508).

Power of Entry

Section 163 carries with it a power of entry under s. 17(1)(c)(iiia) of the Police and Criminal Evidence Act 1984 which states:

> Subject to the following provisions of this section, and without prejudice to any other enactment, a constable may enter and search any premises for the purpose of arresting a person for an offence under . . .
> (iiia) section 4 (driving etc. when under the influence of drink or drugs or section 163 (failure to stop when required to do so by a constable in uniform) of the Road Traffic Act 1988.

The power of entry is only exercisable if the constable has reasonable grounds for believing that the person sought is on the premises (s. 17(2)(a)).

The power to stop vehicles is also available to 'Traffic officers' (Highways Agency Traffic Officers (HATOs) and Welsh Government Traffic Officers (WGTOs)).

There are further powers (under s. 35(1) and (2) of the Road Traffic Act 1988) for a police officer in uniform to stop a vehicle in connection with the regulation of traffic on a road or for the purposes of a road traffic survey carried out on or in the vicinity of a road.

3.2.3 Road Checks

The power to stop vehicles generally is provided under s. 163 of the Road Traffic Act 1988 (officers exercising the power must be in uniform). Having caused a vehicle to stop, there are then certain other powers which may be employed by a police officer (or other authorised people).

Among those powers are the powers set out in the Police and Criminal Evidence Act 1984, s. 4 in relation to 'road checks'.

A road check is where the power under s. 163 of the Road Traffic Act 1988 is used in any locality in such a way as to stop all vehicles or vehicles selected by any criterion (s. 4(2) of the 1984 Act). That general power for uniformed officers to stop vehicles might be used in a particular geographical area to stop all vehicles on the road or all vehicles of a certain make, model or colour, or only those vehicles containing a certain number of adult occupants. In all these cases, there would be a 'road check' for the purposes of s. 4.

The power to carry out road checks following the appropriate authorisation under s. 4 of the Police and Criminal Evidence Act 1984 below is among those that can be conferred on a Police Community Support Officer designated under sch. 4 to the Police Reform Act 2002. In exercising this power, any such officer may also be given the power of a uniformed constable to stop vehicles (under s. 163 of the Road Traffic Act 1988).

The Police and Criminal Evidence Act 1984, s. 4 states:

(1) This section shall have effect in relation to the conduct of road checks by police officers for the purpose of ascertaining whether a vehicle is carrying—
    (a) a person who has committed an offence other than a road traffic offence or a vehicle excise offence;
    (b) a person who is a witness to such an offence;
    (c) a person intending to commit such an offence; or
    (d) a person who is unlawfully at large.
(2) …
(3) Subject to subsection (5) below, there may only be such a road check if a police officer of the rank of superintendent or above authorises it in writing.
(4) An officer may only authorise a road check under subsection (3) above—
    (a) for the purpose specified in subsection (1)(a) above, if he has reasonable grounds—
        (i) for believing that the offence is an indictable offence; and
        (ii) for suspecting that the person is, or is about to be, in the locality in which vehicles would be stopped if the road check were authorised;
    (b) for the purpose specified in subsection (1)(b) above, if he has reasonable grounds for believing that the offence is an indictable offence;
    (c) for the purpose specified in subsection (1)(c) above, if he has reasonable grounds—
        (i) for believing that the offence would be an indictable offence; and
        (ii) for suspecting that the person is, or is about to be, in the locality in which vehicles would be stopped if the road check were authorised;
    (d) for the purpose specified in subsection (1)(d) above, if he has reasonable grounds for suspecting that the person is, or is about to be, in that locality.

KEYNOTE

Road checks may only be authorised for the purposes set out at s. 4(4) and for the duration set out at s. 4(11) (see para. 3.2.3.1).

They must, subject to s. 4(5), be authorised in writing by an officer of superintendent rank or above (s. 4(3)). If it appears to an officer below the rank of superintendent that a road check is required as a matter of urgency for one of the purposes in s. 4(1), he/she may authorise such a road check (s. 4(5)). What amounts to 'urgency' is not defined, but it would appear to be a somewhat subjective requirement based on the apprehension of the officer concerned. Where such an urgent road check is authorised, the authorising officer must, *as soon as is practicable to do so*, make a written record of the time at which the authorisation is given and must cause an officer of superintendent rank or above to be informed of the authorisation (s. 4(6) and (7)). Where this occurs, the superintendent (or more senior officer) may authorise, *in writing*, that the road check continue (s. 4(8)). If the officer considers that the road check should not continue, he/she must make a written record that it took place as well as the purpose for which it took place (including the relevant 'indictable offence' (s. 4(9) and (14)).

The locality in which vehicles are to be stopped must also be specified (s. 4(10)).

Under s. 4(13), every written authorisation for a road check must include:

• the name of the authorising officer;
• the purpose of the road check—including any relevant 'indictable offence';
• the locality in which vehicles are to be stopped.

The road check authorisation also requires the duration of the check to be recorded.

3.2.3.1 Duration of a Road Check

The Police and Criminal Evidence Act 1984, s. 4 goes on to state:

(11) An officer giving an authorisation under this section, other than an authorisation under subsection (5) above—
   (a) shall specify a period, not exceeding seven days, during which the road check may continue; and
   (b) may direct that the road check—
      (i) shall be continuous; or
      (ii) shall be conducted at specified times, during that period.
(12) If it appears to an officer of the rank of superintendent or above that a road check ought to continue beyond the period for which it has been authorised he may, from time to time, in writing specify a further period, not exceeding seven days, during which it may continue.

KEYNOTE

The road check may be extended—in writing—any number of times for further periods up to a total of seven days by a superintendent if it appears to him/her that it 'ought' to continue. There is no restriction of 'reasonableness' or requirement for the existence of particular grounds here and it seems that the judgement may be an entirely subjective one by the superintendent.

Where a vehicle is stopped during a road check, the person in charge of it is entitled to a written statement of the purpose of that road check if he/she applies for one no later than the end of the 12-month period from the day on which the vehicle was stopped (s. 4(15)).

3.2.4 Power to Require the Production of a Driving Licence

The police have access to the DVLA database which allows them to check some aspects of driver records. However, the power to demand that a person, in certain circumstances (e.g. under the fixed penalty system), produce a licence is still valid. Driving licences are dealt with in **chapter 3.9**.

3.2.4.1 Power to Require Production of Driving Licence

The Road Traffic Act 1988, s. 164 states:

(1) Any of the following persons—
   (a) a person driving a motor vehicle on a road,
   (b) a person whom a constable or vehicle examiner has reasonable cause to believe to have been the driver of a motor vehicle at a time when an accident occurred owing to its presence on a road,
   (c) a person whom a constable or vehicle examiner has reasonable cause to believe to have committed an offence in relation to the use of a motor vehicle on a road, or
   (d) a person—
      (i) who supervises the holder of a provisional licence while the holder is driving a motor vehicle on a road, or
      (ii) whom a constable or vehicle examiner has reasonable cause to believe was supervising the holder of a provisional licence while driving, at a time when an accident occurred owing to the presence of the vehicle on a road or at a time when an offence is suspected of having been committed by the holder of the provisional licence in relation to the use of the vehicle on a road,
   must, on being so required by a constable or vehicle examiner, produce his licence for examination, so as to enable the constable or vehicle examiner to ascertain the name and address of the holder of the licence, the date of issue, and the authority by which they were issued.

In order to have met with the requirement to 'produce' a licence the person must allow the constable (or vehicle examiner) a reasonable time to check the name and address of the holder, the date of issue and the authority under which the licence was issued (*Tremelling* v *Martin* [1971] RTR 196). Simply flashing the licence at a police officer or waving it under the officer's nose would not discharge the requirements of s. 164.

The requirement under s. 164(1)(a) is worded in the present tense. Therefore the power to require a licence under this subsection ceases when the driver ceases 'driving' (as to which, **see chapter 3.1**) (*Boyce* v *Absalom* [1974] RTR 248). Unfortunately the legislators did not use the same wording when drafting s. 164(1)(d)(i) in relation to supervisors of learner drivers. It is submitted, however, that the same restrictions would apply and that the power under this section would only apply if the relevant person were still supervising a learner at the time of the demand.

Clearly if a driver is reasonably *believed* to *have been* driving under the circumstances described in s. 164(1)(b), (c) and (d)(ii) then the power to demand the relevant licence would not be restricted to the present tense. It also applies to Community licences (s. 164(11)).

A vehicle examiner is an examiner appointed under s. 66A of the 1988 Act for the purpose of carrying out the functions conferred on them in relation to the Goods Vehicles (Licensing of Operators) Act 1995, the Public Passenger Vehicles Act 1981, the Transport Act 1968 and any other enactment.

Driving licences must be produced in person.

3.2.4.2 Power to Require Date of Birth

The Road Traffic Act 1988, s. 164 states:

> (2) A person required by a constable under subsection (1) above to produce his licence must in pre-scribed circumstances, on being so required by the constable, state his date of birth.

The 'prescribed circumstances' are set out under reg. 83 of the Motor Vehicles (Driving Licences) Regulations 1999 (SI 1999/2864) and are:

- where the person *fails* to produce the licence *forthwith*; *or*
- where the person *produces* a licence which the police officer has reason to suspect:
  - ◆ was not granted to that person;
  - ◆ was granted to that person in error;
  - ◆ contains an alteration to the particulars on the licence *other than the driver number*, made with intent to deceive; or
  - ◆ in which the driver number has been altered, removed or *defaced;* or
- where the person is/was a supervisor of a learner driver as specified under s. 164(1)(d) *and* the police officer has reason to suspect that the person is under 21 years of age.

Failing to state one's date of birth when lawfully required is a summary offence under s. 164(6).

Where a person does state his/her date of birth as required, the Secretary of State may serve a written notice on that person requiring evidence verifying that date of birth. If the person's name differs from his/her name at birth, the Secretary of State may also serve a similar notice requiring a statement from the person as to his/her name when born (s. 164(9)). Knowingly failing to do so is a summary offence (s. 164(9)).

3.2.4.3 Other Driving Licence Powers

Where a police officer has reasonable cause to believe that the holder of a driving licence has knowingly made a false statement to obtain it, the officer may require the production of that licence (s. 164(4)). Failure to do so is a summary offence under s. 164(6).

Where the rider of a motor bicycle produces a provisional driving licence to a police officer and that officer has reasonable cause to believe that the holder was not driving the motor bicycle as part of training on an approved course, the officer may require the production of a prescribed certificate in relation to the completion of, or exemption from, such a course (s. 164(4A)). Failure to produce such a certificate when lawfully required is a summary offence under s. 164(6).

3.2.4.4 Failure to Produce or Deliver Licence

Failing to produce a licence when lawfully required is a summary offence under s. 164(6) of the 1988 Act.

Where a person has had his/her licence revoked in relation to a disability or because it has expired and the licence has not been delivered to the DVLA, a police officer or vehicle examiner may require the licence to be produced and may then seize it (s. 164(3)). Similar powers apply where the licence holder has been ordered to produce his/her licence to a court (s. 164(5)). Failure to do so is a summary offence under s. 164(6).

Licences Surrendered under Fixed Penalty Procedure

If a person has surrendered his/her licence to a police officer in connection with a fixed penalty offence it cannot be produced if required under s. 164. Therefore s. 164(7) provides that, if such a person produces:

- a *current* receipt (under s. 56 of the Road Traffic Offenders Act 1988) to that effect (either then and there or within seven days) and
- *if required to do so*, produces the licence on return to a police station

that person does not commit an offence under s. 164(6).

Defence

The Road Traffic Act 1988, s. 164 states:

(8) In proceedings against any person for the offence of failing to produce a licence it shall be a defence for him to show that—
    (a) within seven days after the production of his licence was required he produced them in person at a police station that was specified by him at the time their production was required, or
    (b) he produced them in person there as soon as was reasonably practicable, or
    (c) it was not reasonably practicable for him to produce them there before the day on which the proceedings were commenced,
and for the purposes of this subsection the laying of the information . . . shall be treated as the commencement of the proceedings.

KEYNOTE

This general defence allows for the issuing of an HORT/1 in respect of driving licences; it also applies to the certificate showing that a licence holder has completed compulsory training in relation to motor bicycles or that the licence holder is exempt from having to complete such a course (s. 164(8A)). Section 164(8) and (8A) also allow for occasions where the production of the relevant documents is not possible at the time.

3.2.5 Power to Require Name and Address/Insurance/Test Certificate

The Road Traffic Act 1988, s. 165 states:

(1) Any of the following persons—
    (a) a person driving a motor vehicle (other than an invalid carriage) on a road, or
    (b) a person whom a constable or vehicle examiner has reasonable cause to believe to have been the driver of a motor vehicle (other than an invalid carriage) at a time when an accident occurred owing to its presence on a road or other public place, or

      (c) a person whom a constable or vehicle examiner has reasonable cause to believe to have committed an offence in relation to the use on a road of a motor vehicle (other than an invalid carriage),

must, on being so required by a constable or vehicle examiner, give his name and address and the name and address of the owner of the vehicle and produce the following documents for examination.

(2) Those documents are—

      (a) the relevant certificate of insurance or certificate of security (within the meaning of Part VI of this Act), or such other evidence that the vehicle is not or was not being driven in contravention of section 143 of this Act as may be prescribed by regulations made by the Secretary of State,

      (b) in relation to a vehicle to which section 47 of this Act applies, a test certificate issued in respect of the vehicle as mentioned in subsection (1) of that section, and

      (c) in relation to a goods vehicle the use of which on a road without a plating certificate or goods vehicle test certificate is an offence under section 53(1) or (2) of this Act, any such certificate issued in respect of that vehicle or any trailer drawn by it.

(2A) Subsections (2B) and (2C) below apply where a certificate of insurance is treated as having been delivered to a person under section 147(1) of this Act by virtue of section 147(1A) of this Act.

(2B) In the case of a certificate transmitted to a person as described in section 147(1A)(a) of this Act, the person is to be treated for the purposes of this section as producing the relevant certificate of insurance if—

      (a) using electronic equipment . . . he provides the constable or examiner with electronic access to a copy of the certificate, or

      (b) he produces a legible printed copy of the certificate.

(2C) In the case of a certificate made available to a person as described in section 147(1A)(b) of this Act, the person is to be treated for the purposes of this section as producing the relevant certificate of insurance if—

      (a) using electronic equipment . . . he provides the constable or examiner with electronic access on the website in question to a copy of the certificate, or

      (b) he produces a legible printed copy of the certificate.

(2D) Nothing in subsection (2B) or (2C) above requires a constable or examiner to provide a person with electronic equipment for the purpose of compliance with a requirement imposed on the person by this section.

(3) Subject to subsection (4) below, a person who fails to comply with a requirement under subsection (1) above is guilty of an offence.

(4) A person shall not be convicted of an offence under subsection (3) above by reason only of failure to produce any certificate or other evidence . . . if in proceedings against him for the offence he shows that—

      (a) within seven days after the date on which the production of the certificate or other evidence was required it was produced at a police station that was specified by him at the time when its production was required, or

      (b) it was produced there as soon as was reasonably practicable, or

      (c) it was not reasonably practicable for it to be produced there before the day on which the proceedings were commenced, and for the purposes of this subsection the laying of the information . . . shall be treated as the commencement of the proceedings.

(5) A person—

      (a) who supervises the holder of a provisional licence granted under Part III of this Act while the holder is driving on a road a motor vehicle (other than an invalid carriage), or

      (b) whom a constable or vehicle examiner has reasonable cause to believe was supervising the holder of such a licence while driving, at a time when an accident occurred owing to the presence of the vehicle on a road or at a time when an offence is suspected of having been committed by the holder of the provisional licence in relation to the use of the vehicle on a road,

must, on being so required by a constable or vehicle examiner, give his name and address and the name and address of the owner of the vehicle.

KEYNOTE

The power to require a name and address in s. 165(1) is among the powers that can be conferred on people (e.g. Police Community Support Officers) designated under schs 4 and 5 to the Police Reform Act 2002 where the suspected offence is one under s. 35 of the Road Traffic Act 1988 (drivers failing to comply with traffic directions).

Production of the certificate need not be in person but the certificate must be shown to the officer for long enough to allow proper inspection of it (as per *Tremelling* at **para. 3.2.4.1, Keynote**).

In cases where a requirement has been made under s. 165, s. 171 of the Road Traffic Act 1988 places a requirement on the *owner* of the vehicle to give such information as required by the police in order to determine whether the motor vehicle was being driven without insurance. Failure to comply with such a requirement is a summary offence.

The requirement under s. 165(1)(b) has been extended to 'public places' as well as roads by the Motor Vehicles (Compulsory Insurance) Regulations 2000 (SI 2000/726).

3.2.6 Power to Seize Vehicles Driven without a Licence or Insurance

The Road Traffic Act 1988 provides powers to seize vehicles in certain circumstances.

Section 165A states that, if *any* of the specified conditions are satisfied in relation to a vehicle, a constable may:

(a) seize the vehicle (in accordance with s. 165A(6) and (7));
(b) remove the vehicle; and
(c) for the purpose of exercising the power, enter any premises other than a private dwelling house on which the constable has reasonable grounds for believing the vehicle to be (s. 165A(1) and (5)).

Note that the definition of 'private dwelling house' does *not* include any garage or other structure occupied with the dwelling house or land 'appurtenant' (belonging or relating) to it.

The first condition is that:

• a constable *in uniform* requires a person to produce his/her driving licence for examination (under s. 164),
• the person fails to produce them, and
• the constable has reasonable grounds for believing that:

a motor vehicle
is or was being driven
by that person
otherwise than in accordance with a licence (in contravention of s. 87(1)).

The second condition is that:

• a constable *in uniform* requires (under s. 165) a person to produce evidence that a motor vehicle is or was not being driven in contravention of s. 143 (requirement for insurance),
• the person fails to produce such evidence, and
• the constable has reasonable grounds for believing that the vehicle is or was being so driven.

The third condition is that:

• a constable *in uniform* requires a person driving a motor vehicle to stop the vehicle (under s. 163),
• the person fails to stop the vehicle, or to stop the vehicle long enough, for the constable to make such lawful inquiries as he/she considers appropriate,
• and the constable has reasonable grounds for believing that:

that vehicle
is or was
being driven
otherwise than in accordance with a licence (in contravention of s. 87(1)) or s.143 (requirement for insurance).

In the exercise of any power to seize a vehicle under this provision or to enter relevant premises, a constable may use reasonable force, if necessary (s. 165A(5)(c)).

However, before seizing the motor vehicle, the constable must warn the person by whom it appears that the vehicle is or was being driven in contravention of s. 87(1) or s. 143 that it will be seized:

(a) in the case of s. 87(1) (driving otherwise than in accordance with a licence) if the person does not produce his/her licence *immediately;*
(b) in the case of s. 143 (no insurance) if the person does not provide the constable *immediately* with evidence that the vehicle is not or was not being driven in contravention of that section.

But the constable is not required to give such a warning if the circumstances make it impracticable to do so (s. 165A(6)).

Section 165A(7) provides that, if the constable is unable to seize the vehicle immediately because the person driving the vehicle has failed to stop as requested or has driven off, it may be seized at any time within the period of 24 hours beginning with the time at which the condition in question is first satisfied. The wording of s. 165A(7) suggests (on one view) that the 24-hour 'window' within which to seize the vehicle only applies where the constable has been prevented from seizing the vehicle immediately owing to the person failing to stop or driving away: it does not therefore apply where some other reason prevented the officer from seizing the vehicle (e.g. by being called away to other duties) in which case there seems to be no restriction on the time during which the vehicle can be seized—ultimately the courts will have to interpret the subsection.

In *Pryor* v *Chief Constable of Greater Manchester* [2011] EWCA Civ 749, the claimant (who did not have his own insurance policy for the vehicle) sued Greater Manchester Police for wrongful interference with goods following their seizure of his car which had been driven by a friend. The friend, who was driving the car with the claimant's permission, was relying on his own insurance policy which contained a clause allowing him to drive, with the consent of the owner, a motor car not owned by, and not hired under a hire purchase or self-drive agreement to, the policyholder. Nonetheless, the officers took the view that the vehicle was uninsured and seized it. The court held they had been wrong to do so and Greater Manchester Police were liable for the wrongful seizure.

A reference to a motor vehicle does not include an invalid carriage (s. 165A(9)).

3.2.6.1 Retention etc. of Vehicles Seized under s. 165A

Under s. 165B the Secretary of State may make regulations providing for the removal and retention of motor vehicles seized under s. 165A and for their release or disposal, together with any fees that may be payable. Those regulations may make different provisions for different cases and will apply to local authorities. So far as England is concerned, local authority means:

• a county council
• the council of a district comprised in an area for which there is no county council
• a London borough council
• the Common Council of the City of London, or
• Transport for London.

In relation to Wales it means the council of a county or county borough.

The relevant regulations are the Road Traffic Act 1988 (Retention and Disposal of Seized Motor Vehicles) Regulations 2005 (SI 2005/1606) and they set out the procedures to be followed by the police in exercising the seizure power.

In summary the regulations provide that:

- When a vehicle has been seized the appropriate police officer (or authorised agent) must take such steps as are reasonably necessary for its safe keeping until it is released or disposed of (reg. 3).
- On seizing a vehicle, the constable must give the driver a seizure notice unless it is impracticable to do so (reg. 4(1)).
- Where the driver is not the owner or registered keeper of the vehicle, the police officer or agent must take reasonably practicable steps to give a seizure notice to the keeper (and to the owner, if that is someone different) unless satisfied that this has already been done or the vehicle has been released in accordance with the regulations (reg. 4(2)).

The seizure notice must give specified details about the seizure and retention of the vehicle including:

- such information as can be (or could have been) ascertained from an inspection of the vehicle, or has been ascertained from any other source, relating to the registration mark and make of the vehicle;
- the place where the vehicle was seized and where it is being kept;
- a requirement that the owner (or keeper) claims it within a specified period of time not being less than seven working days from the day when the notice is given to the registered keeper or owner as the case may be;
- an indication that, unless the vehicle is claimed on or before that date, it may be disposed of; and
- an indication that a person must pay any relevant charges and must produce at a specified police station a valid licence and proof of insurance in respect of his/her use of the vehicle (or nominate a third person who can produce those documents in respect of that person's use of the vehicle to whom the vehicle can be released) (reg. 4(3)–(4)).

Regulation 5 deals with the procedure for releasing a vehicle. If, before a relevant motor vehicle is disposed of, someone:

- satisfies the authorised person that he/she is the registered keeper or the owner of that vehicle;
- pays to the authorised person such a charge in respect of its seizure and retention as provided for in reg. 6; and
- produces at a police station specified in the seizure notice a valid certificate of insurance covering his/her use of that vehicle *and* a valid licence authorising him/her to drive the vehicle,

the authorised person shall permit that person to remove the vehicle.

Specific provision is made for cases where the person claiming the vehicle can demonstrate that he/she is the owner and pays the required fee but nominates a third person who produces a valid certificate of insurance covering his/her use of that vehicle and a valid driving licence authorising him/her to drive that vehicle. In such circumstances, the authorised person must permit that person to remove the vehicle (reg. 5(2)).

Where a vehicle is not released, the conditions under which it can be disposed of are set out in reg. 7. In summary, the vehicle cannot be disposed of until at least 14 days after the date on which the vehicle was seized. If it is sold, the net proceeds are payable to the owner if claimed within a year.

The regulations also provide that the prescribed charges are not payable if the person claiming the vehicle was not driving it at the time of seizure, did not know it was being driven, had not consented to its being driven and could not reasonably have prevented its being driven (reg. 5(5)).

A key feature of the practical arrangements for enforcing the legislation in respect of uninsured drivers is the ability to get relevant information on vehicles and their insured status.

3.2.7   Duty to Give Information as to the Identity of the Driver

The Road Traffic Act 1988, s. 172 states:

(1) This section applies—
   (a) to any offence under the preceding provisions of this Act except—
      (i) an offence under Part V, or
      (ii) an offence under section 13, 16, 51(2), 61(4), 67(9), 68(4), 96 or 120, and to an offence under section 178 of this Act,
   (b) to any offence under sections 25, 26 or 27 of the Road Traffic Offenders Act 1988,
   (c) to any offence against any other enactment relating to the use of vehicles on roads, and
   (d) to manslaughter, or in Scotland culpable homicide, by the driver of a motor vehicle.
(2) Where the driver of a vehicle is alleged to be guilty of an offence to which this section applies—
   (a) the person keeping the vehicle shall give such information as to the identity of the driver as he may be required to give by or on behalf of a chief officer of police, and
   (b) any other person shall if required as stated above give any information which it is in his power to give and may lead to identification of the driver.
(3) Subject to the following provisions, a person who fails to comply with a requirement under sub-section (2) above shall be guilty of an offence.

KEYNOTE

Section 172 applies to offences other than those listed at s. 172(1)(a)–(d). The excepted offences listed at s. 172(1)(a) and (b) are offences relating to:

- driving instructors
- motoring events on public highways
- protective headgear
- testing of goods vehicles
- regulations for 'type approval'
- obstruction of a vehicle examiner
- requirements to proceed to a place of vehicle inspection
- uncorrected eyesight
- regulations for licensing of large goods vehicle/passenger carrying vehicle drivers
- unlawful vehicle taking in Scotland, and
- post-conviction offences under the Road Traffic Offenders Act 1988.

Therefore s. 172 will apply to regulations made under the applicable sections (e.g. the Road Vehicles (Construction and Use) Regulations 1986; see chapter 3.8).

The requirement under s. 172 applies to the person *keeping* the vehicle and will apply to a person who is the keeper of the vehicle at the time the requirement is made even if he/she was not the keeper at the time of the alleged offence (*Hateley* v *Greenough* [1962] Crim LR 329). The second part of the power (s. 172(2)(b)) applies to *any other person*. Failing to give the information is a summary offence punishable by a fine and, in some circumstances, carrying a power for discretionary disqualification. Although it applies to both parts of the power set out above, the relevant offence (under s. 172(3)) creates one single offence (*Mohindra* v *DPP* [2004] EWHC 490 (Admin)).

There is no particular form of words to be used when making the requirement. It must be shown that the person making the requirement did so by, or on behalf of, the chief officer of police. A computerised form stating that the author is so acting has been held by the Divisional Court to be sufficient for this purpose (*Arnold* v *DPP* [1999] RTR 99).

Registered keepers of vehicles captured on roadside speed cameras are frequently served with a statutory notice under s. 172, along with a standard form. The form provides for details of the actual driver to be entered where the recipient of the form was not the driver at the time. If the recipient is unable to provide details of the driver, the form asks for reasons for that inability. Where a registered keeper returned the form with a covering letter stating that he had not completed the form because on the day of the alleged offence more than one person had used the vehicle, he was convicted of failing to comply with the requirement under s. 172. The defendant argued that he had complied with s. 172 because the form only required him to provide details of the actual driver, not a potential driver. The Divisional Court disagreed with him, holding that a notice issued pursuant to s. 172 requires an accurate response and not an inaccurate or misleading statement. That requirement under the notice is carried over to the form. The defendant's claim that he was only required to give details of an actual driver and not a potential driver was clearly contrary to the legislative intention as it would frequently be the case that the registered owner of a vehicle would at least suspect who the driver was, even if he/she did not know for certain, e.g. where the owner lent the vehicle to a friend but was not in the vehicle at the time of the alleged offence (*R (On the Application of Flegg)* v *Southampton and New Forest Justices* [2006] EWHC 396 (Admin)). The High Court has also held, where a husband and wife asserted they did not know which of them drove their Aston Martin at speed through a static camera, that it was not 'on any view irrational for the Magistrates' Court to refuse to exclude the probability that a conscientious and determined enquiry by Mrs Marshall would have revealed whether it was Mrs Marshall or her husband who drove past the agreed camera' when upholding Mrs Marshall's conviction under s. 172(3) (*Marshall* v *CPS* [2015] EWHC 2333 (Admin)).

The information must be provided within a reasonable time which may, in the prevailing circumstances, mean immediately (*Lowe* v *Lester* [1987] RTR 30).

Note that is not necessary for the person to provide the required information on the specific form sent out by the police—it is enough that relevant information is given in writing (*Jones* v *DPP* [2004] EWHC 236 (Admin)).

A chief officer is entitled to require the person providing the information to sign the relevant s. 172 form (*Francis* v *DPP* [2004] EWHC 591 (Admin)).

Where the requirement is made in writing and served by post, it shall have effect as a requirement to provide the information within 28 days beginning with the day on which it is served (s. 172(7)(a)) (see the defence at **para. 3.2.7.1**).

If a person falsely claims to have been the driver, an offence of perverting the course of justice may be appropriate.

Where the defendant is a company or corporate body, any director, secretary, manager or other officer of the company may also be prosecuted for the offence if it can be shown that the offence was committed with his/her 'consent or connivance' (s. 172(5)).

The Divisional Court for England and Wales has confirmed that an admission to being the driver of a particular vehicle given in response to a s. 172 requirement does not breach the defendant's privilege against self-incrimination under Article 6 of the European Convention on Human Rights (*DPP* v *Wilson* [2001] EWHC Admin 198). The court went on to say that, where a defendant disputed the reliability of any such admission, a judge (or magistrate) ought to exercise his/her general discretion to exclude the written evidence and require the prosecution to adduce oral evidence which could then be tested by cross-examination. The court also held that there was no difference, so far as the effect of the Human Rights Act 1998 was concerned, between s. 172(2)(a) and (b).

3.2.7.1 Defence

Section 172(4) provides that a person shall not be convicted of an offence under s. 172(3) if that person can show that he/she did not know *and* could not have ascertained with reasonable diligence who the driver of the vehicle was.

Section 172(7)(b) provides that, where the requirement is made in writing by post, the person shall not be guilty of an offence if that person can show that either he/she gave the information as soon as reasonably practicable after the end of the 28-day period or that it has not been reasonably practicable to give it.

In both of these cases the evidential burden of proof lies on the defendant.

3.3 | Offences Involving Standards of Driving

3.3.1 Introduction

This chapter deals with offences involving driving below the required standard or in a way which presents a danger to others. There are offences here that involve fatal consequences and although all fatalities have a deep impact on those involved this is heightened where the victim is a close friend or relative of the driver (close friend and family cases).

3.3.2 Causing Death by Dangerous Driving

OFFENCE: **Causing Death by Dangerous Driving—*Road Traffic Act 1988, s. 1***
  • Triable on indictment • 14 years' imprisonment • Obligatory disqualification—minimum two years • Compulsory re-test

The Road Traffic Act 1988, s. 1 states:

> A person who causes the death of another person by driving a mechanically propelled vehicle dangerously on a road or other public place is guilty of an offence.

KEYNOTE

For the purposes of this offence, the definition of 'driver' does not include a separate person acting as a steersman.

Note that this offence applies to a 'mechanically propelled vehicle' and can be committed on a road or public place.

Provided the basic elements (mechanically propelled vehicle on a road/public place) are met, you must prove that:

- the defendant caused the death of another person; and
- the defendant drove dangerously.

Where the defendant is charged under s. 1, evidence of drink will be admissible where the quantity of it may have adversely affected the quality of his/her driving (*R* v *Woodward* [1995] RTR 130).

Section 36 of the Road Traffic Offenders Act 1988 (requiring the court to disqualify a person convicted of certain offences until he/she has passed the relevant test) applies to this offence. This means that, if convicted of this offence, the defendant will have to take an extended driving test before getting his/her licence back.

Under the Powers of Criminal Courts (Sentencing) Act 2000, s. 143, forfeiture of the motor vehicle used for the purpose of this offence may be ordered.

3.3.2.1 Causes the Death of Another

The death must be that of a person other than the defendant. This would include a foetus which was later born alive but which subsequently died.

A driver causing the death of another in this way could still be indicted for homicide (*R v Governor of Holloway Prison, ex parte Jennings* [1983] 1 AC 624), however, a charge of manslaughter will rarely be brought in such cases.

The driving by the defendant must be shown to have been *a* cause of the death; it is not necessary to show that it was the sole or even a substantial cause of death (*R v Hennigan* [1971] 3 All ER 133). Therefore it is irrelevant whether or not the person killed contributed to the incident which resulted in his/her death or where it is alleged a second collision was the immediate cause of death (*R v Girdler* [2009] EWCA Crim 2666).

The Court of Appeal has clarified that this offence relates to causing death *by* driving and not causing death *while* driving and therefore the 'driving' does not have to be coextensive with the collision that resulted in the death. In *R v Jenkins* [2012] EWCA Crim 2909 the court held that parking a van to make a delivery, leaving it in conditions of poor visibility where another vehicle collided with it, was certainly a causal link to the fatality that occurred.

3.3.2.2 What is 'Dangerous Driving'?

The Road Traffic Act 1988, s. 2A states:

(1) For the purposes of sections 1, 1A and 2 above a person is to be regarded as driving dangerously if (and, subject to subsection (2) below, only if)—
 (a) the way he drives falls far below what would be expected of a competent and careful driver, and
 (b) it would be obvious to a competent and careful driver that driving in that way would be dangerous.

(2) A person is also to be regarded as driving dangerously for the purposes of sections 1, 1A and 2 above if it would be obvious to a competent and careful driver that driving the vehicle in its current state would be dangerous.

(3) In subsections (1) and (2) above 'dangerous' refers to danger either of injury to any person or of serious damage to property; and in determining for the purposes of those subsections what would be expected of, or obvious to, a competent and careful driver in a particular case, regard shall be had not only to the circumstances of which he could be expected to be aware but also to any circumstances shown to have been within the knowledge of the accused.

(4) In determining for the purposes of subsection (2) above the state of a vehicle, regard may be had to anything attached to or carried on or in it and to the manner in which it is attached or carried.

KEYNOTE

The courts have held that both elements s. 2A(1)(a) and (b) must be demonstrated by the prosecution to prove this element of the offence (*R v Brooks* [2001] EWCA Crim 1944).

This is an objective test which focuses, at s. 2A(1)(a), on the manner of driving rather than the defendant's state of mind and, at s. 2A(1)(b), on what would have been obvious to a hypothetical 'competent and careful driver'. An example is where a diabetic driver drives on a road in the knowledge that he/she is likely to suffer a hypoglycaemic episode (*R v Marison* [1997] RTR 457).

In *Attorney-General's Reference (No. 4 of 2000)* [2001] EWCA Crim 780, the Court of Appeal reviewed the requirements of s. 2A. That case involved a bus driver who had inadvertently pressed the accelerator pedal instead of the brake, killing two pedestrians. The court held that under s. 2A the test is an objective one and there is no requirement to show any specific intent to drive dangerously. It is for the jury to determine what constituted dangerous driving. The court held that the relevant *actus reus* is the act of driving in a manner which was either dangerous (in the case of a dangerous driving charge) or without due care and attention in the case of the alternative offence. Where, as in this case, the driver had been conscious of the act he was performing, it was no defence to claim that he had not intended to press the accelerator. That was more a matter for mitigation than guilt. This view was approved by the Court of Appeal in *R v Shearing* [2012] EWCA Crim 842 where the court recognised that there is an overlap between this offence and that under s. 2B (causing death by careless driving; see para. 3.3.6).

The standard of driving must be shown to have fallen far below that expected of a competent and careful driver; minor driver errors would not amount to such behaviour.

In determining what would have been obvious to a competent and careful driver, s. 2A(3) and (4) introduces a subjective element by taking account of circumstances known to the defendant. This mixture of tests means that, although a defendant's behaviour will be judged against the ordinary standards of competent and careful drivers, the defendant's conduct will also be assessed in the light of facts personally known to him/her (such as knowledge of the risk of a load falling off the vehicle (*R* v *Crossman* [1986] RTR 49)). However, the test is a high one, as confirmed in *R* v *Conteh (Kondeh)* [2003] EWCA Crim 962. In that case the defendant had caused the death of a pedestrian who was crossing the road at a pelican crossing. The lights were red for pedestrians and green for the defendant who was driving at 20 mph in a bus lane. It was shown that the driver of a vehicle in the outside lane had indicated to the pedestrian that she could cross the road. Quashing his conviction under s. 1, the Court of Appeal held that the threshold in s. 2A was a high one and it could not be said that the defendant's driving fell 'far below' the required standard, nor would it have been 'obvious' to a competent and careful driver that it was dangerous. Further, it was good practice expressly to remind a jury that breach of the Highway Code did not necessarily mean that an offence had been committed.

If the vehicle involved was in a dangerous condition it is important that you prove either:

- that the dangerous condition would itself have been obvious to a competent or careful driver; or
- that the defendant actually knew of its dangerous condition.

(*R* v *Strong* [1995] Crim LR 428)

In some circumstances the condition of the driver will be relevant. There are specific offences involving driving while under the influence of drink and/or drugs (**see para. 3.3.5**) and there are several generic road policing offences dealing with drink and drugs (**see chapter 3.5**). However, the mere presence of a controlled drug (such as cocaine) in a driver's blood may of itself be relevant to the issue of whether a person drove dangerously—even if there is no specific evidence as to the drug's effect on the person's driving (*R* v *Pleydell* [2005] EWCA Crim 1447). The fact that a driver was adversely affected by alcohol is a circumstance relevant to the issue of dangerous driving, but is not in itself determinative to prove the offence (*R* v *Webster* [2006] 2 Cr App R 103). There is no requirement to prove whether the defendant was above or below the prescribed limit, as that is not an element of the offence (*R* v *Mari* [2009] EWCA Crim 2677); evidence of the amount of alcohol consumed and said to affect the defendant's ability to drive suffices.

The defendant's belief, however honestly held, as to the conditions surrounding his/her driving at the time is not relevant to the issue of whether he/she drove competently and carefully (*R* v *Collins* [1997] RTR 439). In *Collins* a police driver went through a red traffic light at almost 100 mph colliding with another vehicle and killing two people. His belief that the traffic at the lights was being operated by other officers was not a relevant factor for the jury in considering whether or not his driving had been dangerous.

The CPS 'Policy for prosecuting cases of bad driving' provides a large number of examples of driving behaviour that may support an allegation of dangerous driving. These are indicative only and not conclusive as to the type of behaviour which might constitute dangerous driving. They include:

- Racing or competitive driving.
- Speed which is highly inappropriate for the prevailing road or traffic conditions (although speed alone is not sufficient to found a conviction for dangerous driving (*DPP* v *Milton* [2006] EWHC 242 (Admin)).
- Aggressive driving, such as sudden lane changes, cutting into a line of vehicles or driving much too close to the vehicle in front.
- Disregard of traffic lights and other road signs, which, on an objective analysis, would appear to be deliberate.
- Disregard of warnings from fellow passengers.
- Overtaking that could not have been carried out safely.
- Driving a vehicle with a load that presents a danger to other road users.
- Where the driver is suffering from an impaired ability such as having an arm or leg in plaster, or impaired eyesight.
- Driving when too tired to stay awake.

- Driving a vehicle knowing it has a dangerous defect.
- Using a hand-held mobile phone or other hand-held electronic equipment when the driver was avoidably and dangerously distracted by that use.
- Reading a newspaper/map.
- Talking to and looking at a passenger where the driver was avoidably and dangerously distracted by that.

The dangers presented by dangerous driving mean that there will be many occasions where significant injury is caused to another person by the driving of the vehicle. The Court of Appeal has held that there is nothing wrong in principle in charging a driver with causing grievous bodily harm as well as dangerous driving in appropriate circumstances and that to do so did not amount to an abuse of process (*R* v *Bain* [2005] EWCA Crim 7). However, where a driver was charged with both offences, a court could not impose consecutive terms of imprisonment for both offences arising out of the same incident. With the introduction of the offence of causing serious injury by dangerous driving (**see para. 3.3.3**) the need to charge with both offences may well be consigned to history.

The Court of Appeal gave judgment on the point of whether self-defence was capable of amounting to a defence to a charge of dangerous driving. It concluded that it was; albeit only rarely (*R* v *Tracey Riddell* [2017] EWCA Crim 392).

3.3.2.3 Meaning of Dangerous 'Current State'

The offence may also be committed if the state of a vehicle, including any attachment or load and the way in which it is attached or carried, would make driving it dangerous in the eyes of a 'competent and careful' driver. In relation to the dangerous state of a vehicle being 'obvious', no special definition is required and such an observation could arise from an inspection which is something between a fleeting glance and a long look (*R* v *Marsh* [2002] EWCA Crim 137).

The Court of Appeal has considered the meaning of the term 'current state' of the vehicle. In *R* v *Marchant and Muntz* [2003] EWCA Crim 2099, the court held that the term implied a state different from the original state of the vehicle. In that particular case the vehicle involved had been a tractor fitted with a boom and grab for moving bales. The grab comprised a set of forward-pointing spikes on an upper and lower jaw. With the boom and grab set in the position recommended by the manufacturer, the defendant manoeuvred the tractor to make a turn and, while he waited to do so, a motorcyclist rode into the spikes and later died from his injuries. The defendants were charged with causing death by dangerous driving with the prosecution relying on the s. 2A(2) provision that it would have been obvious to a competent and careful driver that driving the vehicle in its current state would have been dangerous. The defendants argued that the vehicle was an agricultural vehicle specially authorised by the Secretary of State under s. 44 of the Road Traffic Act 1988. The Court of Appeal held that there would be cases where, even though a vehicle was authorised in this way, its condition would allow a prosecution under ss. 1 or 2. However, such cases would almost always involve allegations that the driver had created the danger by manoeuvring the vehicle, rather than simply relying on any danger caused by the vehicle's presence on a road (or other public place). Clearly if the vehicle had been used in a built-up area, or had been altered, allowed to deteriorate or used in a way that contravened the manufacturer's recommendations, the s. 2A argument would have had more force. In the circumstances of the particular case however, the defendants' convictions were quashed.

In a further case involving another tractor the Court of Appeal clarified the extent to which the practice of piling bales of straw onto a trailer would give rise to liability under s. 2. In that case the defendant had been towing a semi-trailer with some 22 bales of straw on it, one of which fell off and seriously injured a pedestrian. The defendant maintained that this 'system of work' had been employed for 25 years without incident and that he had never been warned that it might be unsafe. On the evidence, the court held that it would be perverse to find that the system of carrying bales in this way was inherently 'dangerous' (*R* v *Few* [2005] EWCA Crim 728).

3.3.3 Causing Serious Injury by Dangerous Driving

OFFENCE: **Causing Serious Injury by Dangerous Driving—*Road Traffic Act 1988, s. 1A***

- Triable either way • Five years' imprisonment and/or a fine on indictment
- Six months' imprisonment and/or fine summarily • Obligatory disqualification—minimum two years • Compulsory extended re-test

The Road Traffic Act 1988, s. 1A states:

(1) A person who causes serious injury to another person by driving a mechanically propelled vehicle dangerously on a road or other public place is guilty of an offence.

KEYNOTE

This offence was introduced to the Road Traffic Act 1988 by s. 143 of the Legal Aid, Sentencing and Punishment of Offenders Act 2012. The elements of this offence ('dangerous' and 'dangerous driving') are the same for those under s. 1.

'Serious injury' means physical harm which amounts to grievous bodily harm for the purposes of the Offences Against the Person Act 1861.

The Road Traffic Offenders Act 1988, s. 24, provides an alternative verdict to this offence under the Road Traffic Act 1988, s. 2 (dangerous driving) and s. 3 (careless, and inconsiderate, driving). A person convicted of the offence is subject to a minimum disqualification period of two years, unless the court considers there are special reasons either not to disqualify, or to disqualify for a shorter period. A person convicted of this offence will be disqualified until he/she passes an extended driving test (s. 36 of the Road Traffic Offenders Act 1988).

Under the Powers of Criminal Courts (Sentencing) Act 2000, s. 143, forfeiture of the motor vehicle used for the purpose of this offence may be ordered.

3.3.4 Dangerous Driving

OFFENCE: **Dangerous Driving—*Road Traffic Act 1988, s. 2***

- Triable either way • Two years' imprisonment and/or a fine on indictment
- Six months' imprisonment and/or statutory maximum summarily
- Obligatory disqualification • Compulsory re-test

The Road Traffic Act 1988, s. 2 states:

A person who drives a mechanically propelled vehicle dangerously on a road or other public place is guilty of an offence.

KEYNOTE

The elements of this offence are the same as those for s. 1.

Evidence showing how the particular vehicle was being driven before the incident itself may be given in support of the charge of dangerous driving. However, care needs to be taken by the prosecution not to seek to adduce inadmissible evidence about the defendant's past bad driving (*R* v *McKenzie* [2008] EWCA Crim 758). Where the dangerous driving leads to a collision, the court may allow a police officer who is an expert in the investigation of collisions to give evidence of opinion as to the cause of that collision (*R* v *Oakley* [1979] RTR 417).

In addition, there is a rarely used offence of causing bodily harm by wanton or furious driving or racing (Offences Against the Person Act 1861, s. 35) which is punishable by two years' imprisonment.

Section 36 of the Road Traffic Offenders Act 1988 (requiring the court to disqualify a person convicted of certain offences until the relevant test has been passed) applies to this offence. This means that, if convicted of this offence, the defendant will have to take an extended driving test before getting his/her licence back.

3.3.5 Causing Death by Careless Driving when under the Influence of Drink or Drugs

OFFENCE: **Causing Death by Careless Driving when under the Influence of Drink or Drugs—*Road Traffic Act 1988, s. 3A***

• Triable on indictment • 14 years' imprisonment • Obligatory disqualification—minimum two years

The Road Traffic Act 1988, s. 3A states:

(1) If a person causes the death of another person by driving a mechanically propelled vehicle on a road or other public place without due care and attention, or without reasonable consideration for other persons using the road or place, and—

    (a) he is, at the time when he is driving, unfit to drive through drink or drugs, or

    (b) he has consumed so much alcohol that the proportion of it in his breath, blood or urine at that time exceeds the prescribed limit, or

    (ba) he has in his body a specified controlled drug and the proportion of it in his blood or urine at that time exceeds the specified limit for that drug, or

    (c) he is, within 18 hours after that time, required to provide a specimen in pursuance of section 7 of this Act, but without reasonable excuse fails to provide it, or

    (d) he is required by a constable to give his permission for a laboratory test of a specimen of blood taken from him under section 7A of this Act, but without reasonable excuse fails to do so,

    he is guilty of an offence.

(2) For the purposes of this section a person shall be taken to be unfit to drive at any time when his ability to drive properly is impaired.

(3) Subsection (1)(b) (ba) (c) and (d) above shall not apply in relation to a person driving a mechanically propelled vehicle other than a motor vehicle.

KEYNOTE

There are a number of different ways that this offence can be committed. The prosecution need to establish that:

• the accused was driving without due care and attention; or

• without reasonable consideration for other persons using the road or place, and at that time:

• was unfit to drive through drink or drugs; or

• had consumed so much alcohol that the proportion of it in his breath, blood or urine at that time exceeded the prescribed limit; or

• had in his body a specified controlled drug and the proportion of it in his blood or urine at that time exceeded the specified limit for that drug; or

• within 18 hours after that time, the accused was required to provide a specimen in pursuance of s. 7 of the Road Traffic Act 1988, but without reasonable excuse fails to provide it; or

• he is required by a constable to give his permission for a laboratory test of a specimen of blood taken from him under s. 7A of the 1988 Act, but without reasonable excuse fails to do so,

and

• the death of another person was caused by the manner of his driving.

The elements in relation to 'causes the death of another person' are the same as those under s. 1.

The elements relating to 'due care and attention' and 'reasonable consideration' are discussed at **para. 3.3.6.1**.

The elements relating to unfitness to drive and being over the prescribed limit for alcohol or drugs are the same as those contained in drink drive legislation in **chapter 3.5**. For this offence this means that s. 3A(1)(b) (ba), (c) and (d) apply only where the driving is of a 'motor vehicle', but the offence under s. 3A(1)(a) may be committed while driving any 'mechanically propelled vehicle'.

Effectively the prosecution would therefore have to prove careless driving and the related 'drink/drug driving' offence in exactly the same way as if both offences had been charged, together with the requisite causal link to the death. The offence, however, does not require any causal connection between the alcohol or drugs and the death (*R* v *Shepherd* [1994] 1 WLR 530).

In applying the appropriate test to determine whether the defendant has driven without due care and attention, the jury are entitled to look at all the circumstances of the case, including evidence that the defendant had been affected by alcohol or had taken such an amount of alcohol as would be likely to affect a driver (*R* v *Millington* [1996] RTR 80).

The requirement under s. 3A(1)(c) is for the provision of a specimen for analysis under s. 7 of the Road Traffic Act 1988 and not a screening test under s. 6.

The wording in s. 3A(1)(c) seems to indicate that the request to provide a specimen must be made within 18 hours after the driving which caused the death and not after the death itself.

Section 36 of the Road Traffic Offenders Act 1988 (requiring the court to disqualify a person convicted of certain offences until the relevant test has been passed) applies to this offence. This means that, if convicted of this offence, the defendant will have to take an extended driving test before getting his/her licence back.

3.3.6 Causing Death by Careless, or Inconsiderate, Driving

OFFENCE: **Causing Death by Careless or Inconsiderate Driving—*Road Traffic Act 1988*, s. 2B**
- Triable either way • Five years' imprisonment and/or a fine on indictment
- 12 months' imprisonment (six months in Scotland) and/or statutory maximum summarily • Obligatory disqualification

The Road Traffic Act 1988, s. 2B states:

A person who causes the death of another person by driving a mechanically propelled vehicle on a road or other public place without due care and attention, or without reasonable consideration for other persons using the road or place, is guilty of an offence.

KEYNOTE

The elements in relation to 'causes the death of another person' are the same as those under s. 1.

This section was added to bridge the large gap between causing death by dangerous driving and careless driving that resulted in a death. There will clearly be an overlap between the driving standards of this offence and that of causing death by dangerous driving, a fact the courts have recognised (see *Shearing* at **para. 3.3.2.2**, **Keynote**).

3.3.6.1 What is 'Careless and Inconsiderate' Driving?

A person is to be regarded as driving without due care and attention if (and only if) the way he/she drives falls below what would be expected of a competent and careful driver (s. 3ZA(2)).

As with dangerous driving, the test is entirely objective in nature and focuses on the manner of driving rather than the defendant's state of mind. The element that distinguishes dangerous driving from careless driving is that the dangerous driver falls *far below* the required standard while the careless driver merely falls *below* the required standard (**see para. 3.3.2.2**, **Keynote**).

Note also that if the defendant is alleged to have driven without reasonable consideration for another road user, that other road user must *actually* be inconvenienced by the defendant's driving; it is not enough that there was potential for inconvenience (s. 3ZA(4)).

There is one *objective* standard of driving which is expected of all drivers, including learner drivers (*McCrone* v *Riding* [1938] 1 All ER 157) (**see para. 3.9.4**). Once you have proved that a defendant departed from that standard of driving, and that the defendant's actions were 'voluntary', the offence is complete. There is no need to prove any *knowledge* or *awareness* by the defendant that his/her driving fell below that standard (*R* v *Lawrence* [1982] AC 510).

The standard of driving that would be expected of a competent and careful driver will be a question of fact for the court to decide and, in so deciding, the magistrate(s) may take into account local factors such as the expected level of traffic, the time of day, peculiar hazards, etc. (*Walker* v *Tolhurst* [1976] RTR 513).

The Administrative Court has accepted that a distraction (such as children on the carriageway) can amount to a defence to a charge of careless driving (*Plunkett* v *DPP* [2004] EWHC 1937 (Admin)). However, each case will turn on its own facts and a court may nevertheless find that the nature or extent of the distraction does not absolve the driver from the consequences of not paying sufficient attention (e.g. by concentrating for too long on the distraction itself when considered in light of the speed of the vehicle and the nature of other hazards on the road).

Other persons using the road/public place can include pedestrians who are deliberately sprayed with water from a puddle or passengers in a vehicle (*Pawley* v *Wharldall* [1966] 1 QB 373).

3.3.7 Causing Death by Driving: Unlicensed, Disqualified or Uninsured Drivers

OFFENCE: **Causing Death by Driving: Unlicensed or Uninsured Drivers—*Road Traffic Act 1988*, s. 3ZB**
- Triable either way • Two years' imprisonment and/or a fine on indictment
- 12 months' imprisonment and/or statutory maximum summarily
- Obligatory disqualification

The Road Traffic Act 1988, s. 3ZB states:

A person is guilty of an offence under this section if he causes the death of another person by driving a motor vehicle on a road and, at the time when he is driving, the circumstances are such that he is committing an offence under—
  (a) section 87(1) of this Act (driving otherwise than in accordance with a licence), or
  (b) ...
  (c) section 143 of this Act (using motor vehicle while uninsured or unsecured against third party risks).

KEYNOTE

The elements in relation to 'causing the death of' and 'another person' are, generally, the same as those under s. 1.

This offence was initially construed as a 'but for' offence. It was considered that a person who should not have been on the road as they were disqualified, had no insurance or no driving licence ought to have their presence 'punished' where a fatality occurred. It was considered that 'but for' the presence of this person on that road, who indeed should not have been there, at that time a fatality may not have occurred and converted the basic offence to a far more serious one. This was confirmed by the Court of Appeal in *R* v *Williams* [2010] EWCA Crim 2552 where the deceased walked directly into the path of the uninsured defendant's car. The conviction was upheld despite the lack of any fault in the quality of the defendant's driving.

However the Supreme Court has now ruled that there must be something more than 'but for' causation. In *R* v *Hughes* [2013] UKSC 56 their lordships made clear that the 'but for' interpretation 'confuses criminal responsibility for the serious offence of being uninsured with criminal responsibility for the infinitely more serious offence of killing another person'.

In terms of directions to the jury where such an offence is charged:

...it is not necessary for the Crown to prove careless or inconsiderate driving, but...there must be something open to proper criticism in the driving of the defendant, beyond the mere presence of the vehicle on the road, and which contributes in some more than minimal way to the death.

This offence may only be committed by the driver of a *motor vehicle* (not a mechanically propelled vehicle unlike ss. 2, 2B and 3).

OFFENCE: **Causing Death by Driving: Disqualified Drivers—*Road Traffic***
Act 1988, s. 3ZC

- Triable on indictment • 10 years' imprisonment and/or a fine
- Obligatory disqualification

The Road Traffic Act 1988, s. 3ZC states:

A person is guilty of an offence under this section if he or she—
  (a) causes the death of another person by driving a motor vehicle on a road, and
  (b) at that time, is committing an offence under section 103(1)(b) of this Act (driving while disqualified).

OFFENCE: **Causing Serious Injury by Driving: Disqualified Drivers—*Road Traffic***
Act 1988, s. 3ZD

- Triable either way • Four years' imprisonment and/or a fine on indictment
- 12 months' imprisonment and/or fine summarily • Obligatory disqualification

The Road Traffic Act 1988, s. 3ZD states:

A person is guilty of an offence under this section if he or she—
  (a) causes serious injury to another person by driving a motor vehicle on a road, and
  (b) at that time, is committing an offence under section 103(1)(b) of this Act (driving while disqualified)...

KEYNOTE

The introduction of s. 3ZC is to increase the sentence for causing death driving a vehicle whilst disqualified from two years to 10 years. The intention is to treat disqualified drivers differently from other illegal drivers.

This section, in relation to disqualified drivers who 'cause' death or serious injury, must be read in the light of the Supreme Court judgment in *Hughes* above.

Section 3ZD extends the offence under s. 1A of causing serious injury by dangerous driving specifically to disqualified drivers, increasing the sentence to four years' imprisonment from the six months' imprisonment under s. 1A and removing the need to show 'dangerous' driving. In this section 'serious injury' means physical harm which amounts to grievous bodily harm for the purposes of the Offences Against the Person Act 1861.

3.3.8 Careless and Inconsiderate Driving

OFFENCE: **Careless and Inconsiderate Driving—*Road Traffic Act 1988, s. 3***

- Triable summarily • Fine • Discretionary disqualification

The Road Traffic Act 1988, s. 3 states:

If a person drives a mechanically propelled vehicle on a road or other public place without due care and attention, or without reasonable consideration for other persons using the road or place, he is guilty of an offence.

KEYNOTE

The elements in relation to 'due care and attention' are discussed at para. 3.3.6.1.

Where a constable in uniform has reasonable grounds for believing that a mechanically propelled vehicle is being used or has been used on any occasion in a manner which contravenes s. 3 or 34 (off-road driving) and is causing (or is likely to cause) alarm, distress or annoyance to members of the public, the constable has the powers set out in the Police Reform Act 2002, s. 59 (as to which, see para. 3.7.9).

3.3.8.1 Factors Affecting Offence of Careless Driving

Evidence of earlier incidents involving careless or inconsiderate driving around the same time as the offence charged may be admissible to support that charge under some circumstances (*Hallett* v *Warren* (1926) 93 JP 225) as it may if the offence is charged as one continuing offence (*Horrix* v *Malam* [1984] RTR 112).

If a witness reports the driver of an unidentified vehicle as having committed a driving offence, it is critical that the witness provides direct evidence of what he/she actually saw. It would not be enough to produce evidence from the police to show that they had received details of the vehicle which they subsequently traced back to the driver. Both vehicle *and* driver must be linked by admissible and relevant evidence (*Ahmed* v *DPP* [1998] RTR 90).

If a driver falls asleep at the wheel he/she will be guilty of careless driving (*Henderson* v *Jones* (1955) 119 JP 304) but evidence of this fact from the driver alone will not be enough to support a charge under s. 3 (*Edwards* v *Clarke* (1951) 115 JPN 426).

Responding to an Emergency Situation

If a motorist takes action in response to an emergency situation, his/her actions are to be judged against what was a 'reasonable' course of action in those circumstances in assessing whether or not the driving amounted to an offence (*R* v *Bristol Crown Court, ex parte Jones* [1986] RTR 259).

Relevance of Breaching Road Traffic Regulations

Breaching certain road traffic regulations will always be potentially relevant evidence of poor driving but will not always be conclusive of the issue. For instance, although colliding with another vehicle has been held not to amount to sufficient evidence in itself of careless driving, crossing a central white line without explanation has (*Mundi* v *Warwickshire Police* [2001] EWHC 448 (Admin)). (See also *Bensley* v *Smith* [1972] Crim LR 239.) However, simply breaching the regulations at a pedestrian crossing is not of itself proof that the person's driving fell below the required standard (*Gibbons* v *Kahl* [1956] 1 QB 59). On the other hand, just because a traffic signal is showing a green light does not mean that a driver is entitled to assume that no other person or vehicle might be proceeding from another direction and it may be that, in the circumstances, a reasonably careful driver would have anticipated that a pedestrian or other road user might still move into his/her path (*Goddard and Walker* v *Greenwood* [2002] EWCA Civ 1590).

3.3.9 The Highway Code

One way of illustrating the standard of driving expected of a prudent and competent driver is through the Highway Code. Section 38 of the Road Traffic Act 1988 states:

> (7) A failure on the part of a person to observe a provision of the Highway Code shall not of itself render that person liable to criminal proceedings of any kind but any such failure may in any proceedings (whether civil or criminal, and including proceedings for an offence under the Traffic Acts, the Public Passenger Vehicles Act 1981 or sections 18 to 23 of the Transport Act 1985) be relied upon by any party to the proceedings as tending to establish or negative any liability which is in question in those proceedings.

KEYNOTE

The Highway Code gives motorists and road users guidance on all manner of practical and safety issues, and in particular advice in relation to considerate driving and the proper use of headlights, horns and indicators. The Code also gives advice on police stopping procedures. The provisions of the Highway Code, while certainly not conclusive, may still merit careful consideration as guidance as to the standards to be attributed to a competent and careful driver (*R* v *Taylor* [2004] EWCA Crim 213).

However, as the Court of Appeal has reminded us, breach of the Highway Code does not necessarily mean that an offence has been committed (*R* v *Conteh (Kondeh)* [2003] EWCA Crim 962).

The braking distances shown in the Highway Code however are not admissible in proving speeding cases as they amount to hearsay (*R* v *Chadwick* [1975] Crim LR 105).

3.3.10 Dangerous, Careless and Inconsiderate Cycling

There are similar offences which regulate the standard of cycling on *roads*. These are found under ss. 28 and 29 of the Road Traffic Act 1988 and are summary offences punishable with a fine. The offence of causing bodily injury by 'furious driving' also applies to pedal cycles.

'Cycles' will include tricycles and any cycle having four or more wheels (s. 192 of the 1988 Act).

3.3.11 Refusing to Give Details

OFFENCE: **Refusing to Give, or Giving False Details after Allegation of Dangerous or Careless Driving or Cycling—*Road Traffic Act 1988, s. 168***
- Triable summarily • Fine

The Road Traffic Act 1988, s. 168 states:

Any of the following persons—
   (a) the driver of a mechanically propelled vehicle who is alleged to have committed an offence under section 2 or 3 of this Act, or
   (b) the rider of a cycle who is alleged to have committed an offence under section 28 or 29 of this Act who refuses, on being so required by any person having reasonable ground for so requiring, to give his name or address, or gives a false name or address, is guilty of an offence.

KEYNOTE

This requirement arises where the driver (or rider) is alleged to have committed an offence of dangerous or careless driving or cycling.

There is no requirement for an accident of any sort to have occurred.

The section uses the word 'refuses' but makes no mention of a *failure* to provide the required details. Although s. 11(2) of the 1988 Act makes provision for a 'failure' to include a 'refusal' (in relation to drink driving offences), the Act says nothing about a *vice versa* situation. Given that omission, together with the fact that the courts have held (albeit in an employment law case) that 'failure' is not synonymous with 'refusal' (*Lowson* v *Percy Main & District Social Club and Institute Ltd* [1979] ICR 568), it would seem that a mere failure to provide the details required under s. 168 will not amount to the offence above.

3.4 Reportable Accidents

3.4.1 Introduction

There are certain provisions that relate to 'reportable' accidents and these, rather than the causes, are the subject of this chapter.

3.4.2 Duty of Driver

The Road Traffic Act 1988, s. 170 states:

(1) This section applies in a case where, owing to the presence of a mechanically propelled vehicle on a road or other public place, an accident occurs by which—
    (a) personal injury is caused to a person other than the driver of that mechanically propelled vehicle, or
    (b) damage is caused—
        (i) to a vehicle other than that mechanically propelled vehicle or a trailer drawn by that mechanically propelled vehicle, or
        (ii) to an animal other than an animal in or on that mechanically propelled vehicle or a trailer drawn by that mechanically propelled vehicle, or
        (iii) to any other property constructed on, fixed to, growing in or otherwise forming part of the land on which the road or place in question is situated or land adjacent to such land.
(2) The driver of the mechanically propelled vehicle must stop and, if required to do so by any person having reasonable grounds for so requiring, give his name and address and also the name and address of the owner and the identification marks of the vehicle.
(3) If for any reason the driver of the mechanically propelled vehicle does not give his name and address under subsection (2) above, he must report the accident.
(4) . . .
(5) If, in a case where this section applies by virtue of subsection (1)(a) above, the driver of a motor vehicle does not at the time of the accident produce such a certificate of insurance or security, or other evidence, as is mentioned in section 165(2)(a) of this Act—
    (a) to a constable, or
    (b) to some person who, having reasonable grounds for so doing, has required him to produce it, the driver must report the accident and produce such a certificate or other evidence.
    This subsection does not apply to the driver of an invalid carriage.
(6) To comply with a duty under this section to report an accident or to produce such a certificate of insurance or security, or other evidence, as is mentioned in section 165(2)(a) of this Act, the driver—
    (a) must do so at a police station or to a constable, and
    (b) must do so as soon as is reasonably practicable and, in any case, within twenty-four hours of the occurrence of the accident.
(7) . . .
(8) In this section 'animal' means horse, cattle, ass, mule, sheep, pig, goat or dog.

KEYNOTE

This duty applies to accidents on a road or a public place. This addition was unsuccessfully contested in the courts (*R (On the Application of Parker)* v *Crown Court at Bradford* [2006] EWHC 3213 (Admin)).

Accidents as defined under s. 170(1)(a) and (b) are generally referred to as 'reportable' accidents. If the *only* person injured is the *driver* of the mechanically propelled vehicle concerned, the accident will not be reportable. Similarly, if the only damage caused is to the mechanically propelled vehicle or trailer drawn thereby or to an animal in the mechanically propelled vehicle or trailer drawn thereby, the accident will not fall within the criteria of being 'reportable'.

A 'trailer' is defined under s. 185(1) of the Road Traffic Act 1988 as a vehicle drawn by a motor vehicle. When a motor vehicle is towed by another motor vehicle, the latter still falls within the category of motor vehicle but can also be regarded as a 'trailer' (*Milstead* v *Sexton* [1964] Crim LR 474).

Damage caused under the circumstances set out at s. 170(1)(b) applies to any vehicle (such as bicycles (*Ellis* v *Nott-Bower* (1896) 60 JP 760)) and not just one which is mechanically propelled.

No mention is made of who may have been to blame for the accident as drivers will attract the duties even if they are not at fault. In order to attract those duties, however, the driver must know of the accident (*Harding* v *Price* [1948] 1 KB 695). In proving the offence you would not have to show that the driver was so aware; once the damage or injury is proved it is for drivers to show (on the balance of probabilities) that they were unaware of its occurrence (*Selby* v *Chief Constable of Avon and Somerset* [1988] RTR 216). The Divisional Court has held that a driver cannot rely on the fact they were drunk as to whether they were aware an accident had occurred or not. The court stated that even if it could properly find that the appellant was unaware of the accident because of their drunken state, they could not rely upon that as a defence. The defendant would have been able to rely on it had they been sober, but not where they were voluntarily intoxicated (*Magee* v *Crown Prosecution Service* [2014] EWHC 4089 (Admin)).

The obligations created by the Act fall on the 'driver' and the 'driver' alone—not the driver's agent or employee. The 'driver' may still be under the obligations imposed by s. 170 if an accident occurs while he/she is away from the vehicle (see *Cawthorn* at para. 3.1.6).

The accident must have been brought about owing to the vehicle's presence on a 'road' or other public place; therefore s. 170 does not apply to accidents which occur purely on private premises. However, where the accident results from driving where the mechanically propelled vehicle has run off a road and collided with some stationary object, this is an accident which occurred 'owing to the presence of a mechanically propelled vehicle on a road' (*R* v *Stapylton* [2012] EWCA Crim 728).

3.4.2.1 Stop

Stop under s. 170(2) means to stop safely and remain at the scene for such a time as would allow anyone having a right or reason for doing so to ask for information from the driver (*Lee* v *Knapp* [1967] 2 QB 442). This duty also appears to require the driver to stay with the vehicle for a reasonable time (*Ward* v *Rawson* [1978] RTR 498). What a 'reasonable time' is will be a question of fact and degree—it depends where the accident occurred and in what conditions and the duty does not require drivers to make inquiries of their own to try to find such a person (*Mutton* v *Bates* [1984] RTR 256).

Where a bus driver braked hard, causing injury to one of his passengers, the Divisional Court held that he had a duty to stop at the place and the time that the passenger was caused to be injured. It was not open to the driver to claim that the bus itself was the scene of the accident. The fact that the driver failed to stop immediately meant that he was guilty of an offence under s. 170(4) (*Hallinan* v *DPP* [1998] Crim LR 754).

Whether or not the vehicle is stopped at the appropriate point is a question of fact; where a driver chose to drive on for 80 yards before stopping and returning to the scene of the accident, the Divisional Court was not prepared to interfere with a decision finding that this constituted a failure to stop as required (*McDermott* v *DPP* [1997] RTR 474). The offence is complete as soon as the failure to stop occurs.

3.4.2.2 Providing Details

'Damage Only' Accident

The driver of the mechanically propelled vehicle involved in a damage only accident must, if required to do so, provide:

- his/her name and address;
- the name and address of the owner of the vehicle; and
- the identification marks of the vehicle.

A failure to provide any or all of these details, *if required to do so (i.e. if someone asked for them)*, would constitute an offence under s. 170(4). A failure to provide any details because they have not been requested, e.g. because nobody asks for them or nobody is at the scene of the accident, would not constitute an offence. However, if, *for any reason whatsoever*, the driver does not provide his/her name and address to anyone, the driver must report the accident to the police.

It has been held that, as the reason for this requirement to 'exchange details' is to allow future communications between interested parties, the address of the driver's solicitor (rather than the driver's address) would be enough to discharge the duty at s. 170(2) (*DPP* v *McCarthy* [1999] RTR 323).

Injury Accident

The driver of the mechanically propelled vehicle involved in a personal injury accident must, if required to do so, provide:

- his/her name and address;
- the name and address of the owner of the vehicle;
- the identification marks of the vehicle; and
- his/her insurance/security details (which can be provided to a constable or to the person having reasonable grounds for requiring it).

A failure to provide any or all of these details, *if required to do so (i.e. if someone asked for them)*, would constitute an offence under s. 170(4) and (7). Once again, a failure to provide any details because they were not requested for some reason would not constitute an offence. However, if, *for any reason whatsoever*, the driver does not provide his/her name and address AND insurance/security details to anyone (e.g. because the driver refused to give the details or there was nobody to give the details to), the driver must report the accident to the police.

3.4.2.3 Injury

Injury must occur to someone other than the driver of the mechanically propelled vehicle. Injury to a passenger in the vehicle would suffice. Under s. 170 injury has been held to include shock and it would appear that psychological harm may well amount to an 'injury' for these purposes.

3.4.2.4 Duty to Report

If the driver does not give his/her details (driver's name and address when involved in a damage-only accident or when involved in an injury accident his/her driver's name and address and insurance/security details), the accident must be reported to a police officer or at a police station. It does *not* matter what the reason for non-provision of the information is. The report must be made as soon as reasonably practicable (which will be a question of fact for the court to decide in each circumstance) and in any case within 24 hours of the occurrence of the incident. This latter requirement does not give the driver up to 24 hours to report the accident; that report must be made as soon as is reasonably practicable.

In *Bulman* v *Lakin* [1981] RTR 1 the defendant had an accident at 1.10am, and at 11am, after a police constable had fruitlessly called three times at the home of the defendant, he called in and reported the accident at a police station. The Divisional Court held that the offence was made out.

That duty was not discharged when the driver waited until the police called at his house and then only told them as a result of their coming to interview him (*Dawson* v *Winter*

(1932) 49 TLR 128 *obiter*); neither is it discharged if the driver informs a police officer as a friend and not in the capacity of a police officer (*Mutton* v *Bates* [1984] RTR 256).

Any report must be made in person; telephoning (and presumably sending a fax or email to) a police station is not enough (*Wisdom* v *McDonald* [1983] RTR 186).

Section 170 imposes a clear obligation on the driver of a vehicle involved in an accident resulting in damage or injury to report the accident to the police. That requirement is not negated either by police attendance at the accident or by the driver being taken to hospital (*DPP* v *Hay* [2005] EWHC 1395 (Admin)).

3.4.3 The Offences

OFFENCE: **Failing to Stop/Report an Accident/Give Information or Documents— Road Traffic Act 1988, s. 170(4)**
 • Triable summarily • Six months' imprisonment and/or a fine • Discretionary disqualification

The Road Traffic Act 1988, s. 170 states:

(4) A person who fails to comply with subsections (2) or (3) above is guilty of an offence.

OFFENCE: **Failing to Produce Proof of Insurance after Injury Accident—*Road Traffic Act 1988, s. 170(7)***
 • Triable summarily • Fine

The Road Traffic Act 1988, s. 170 states:

(7) A person who fails to comply with a duty under subsection (5)...guilty of an offence, but he shall not be convicted by reason only of a failure to produce a certificate or other evidence if, within seven days after the occurrence of the accident, the certificate or other evidence is produced at a police station that was specified by him at the time when the accident was reported.

KEYNOTE

The wording of s.170(2) and (3) means that if a driver fails to stop *and* fails to report an accident, *two* offences are committed that of failing to stop and later failing to report (*Roper* v *Sullivan* [1978] RTR 181).

The Court of Appeal refused to accept that a driver who failed to stop and report an accident for fear of being breathalysed did not, without more, commit an offence of perverting the course of justice (*R* v *Clark* [2003] EWCA Crim 991). While it is true that driving home and remaining there allowed the passage of time to dissipate the level of alcohol in the driver's body and thereby avoid conviction for a drink driving offence (as to which, **see chapter 3.5**), the court was not convinced that this was enough to justify being charged with such a serious offence as this would be a 'large leap' not a case-by-case basis in relation to precedents.

3.5 | Drink, Drugs and Driving

3.5.1 Introduction

The law regulating drinking and driving is contained in the Road Traffic Act 1988 and the Road Traffic Offenders Act 1988.

Although what follows in this chapter is a discussion of some of the relevant law and powers of enforcement, there is an increasing emphasis on judicial action to prevent re-offending. Sections 34A to 34C of the Road Traffic Offenders Act 1988 allow drink-drive offenders who are disqualified from driving to have the period of disqualification reduced if they complete a drink-drive rehabilitation course. These reductions in the disqualification period must be not less than three months, and not more than one quarter of the unreduced period (this equates to a new, reduced, disqualification period of between three and nine months for a 12-month sentence).

A further scheme designed to emphasise the safety considerations in driving while unfit or over the prescribed limit is the High Risk Offender (HRO) scheme. This scheme generally applies to offenders who are convicted of relevant offences and at the time were either more than 2½ times the prescribed limit or for whom the conviction is their second (or more) in 10 years. Under the scheme, these offenders will be required to take a medical test before being allowed to regain their drivers' licence at the end of their period of disqualification and they must effectively satisfy the licensing authority that they do not have a serious alcohol problem.

It should be noted that the Road Traffic Act 1988 makes reference to the availability *in law* of a device enabling what is termed as a 'roadside *evidential* specimen of breath' (not to be confused with a preliminary roadside *screening* test) to be obtained. The idea is that an evidential specimen could be obtained by an approved device *at the roadside or even at a hospital* rather than at a police station. This might occur, for example, immediately after a positive screening test has taken place (see s. 7(2)(c) at **para. 3.5.5.1**). This would limit the opportunity to escape a conviction for an offence committed under s. 5 (over the prescribed limit) because of the amount of time elapsed between the positive screening test and the evidential specimen being obtained at a police station. While the legislation that created and governs the use of such a device (the Serious Organised Crime and Police Act 2005) has been in force for some time, it is important to stress that no device is currently available for operational use. The only devices currently used to obtain an evidential specimen of breath are those situated at a police station (Lion or Camic device). However, as the provisions relating to these devices are an integral part of the Road Traffic Act 1988, they are dealt with within this chapter in order to provide the reader with the most complete picture of the current *legislative framework* that exists in relation to drink/drive matters.

3.5.2 Unfit through Drink or Drugs

OFFENCE: **Driving or Attempting to Drive a Mechanically Propelled Vehicle when Unfit through Drink or Drugs—*Road Traffic Act 1988, s. 4(1)***
- • Triable summarily • Six months' imprisonment and/or a fine • Obligatory disqualification

The Road Traffic Act 1988, s. 4 states:

(1) A person who, when driving or attempting to drive a mechanically propelled vehicle on a road or other public place, is unfit to drive through drink or drugs is guilty of an offence.

OFFENCE: **Being in Charge of a Mechanically Propelled Vehicle when Unfit through Drink or Drugs—*Road Traffic Act 1988, s. 4(2)***

• Triable summarily • Three months' imprisonment and/or a fine • Discretionary disqualification

The Road Traffic Act 1988, s. 4 states:

(2) Without prejudice to subsection (1) above, a person who, when in charge of a mechanically propelled vehicle which is on a road or other public place, is unfit to drive through drink or drugs is guilty of an offence.

KEYNOTE

Section 4 creates three separate offences. For the definitions of 'driving', 'attempting to drive' and 'in charge' and the other relevant terms used in this offence, **see chapter 3.1**.

It will not be enough to rely on a *suspicion* that the defendant *had been driving* in order to prove the offence. Suspicion may be enough to trigger powers to require preliminary tests or powers of entry; it will not however be enough to prove the required element of driving/attempting to drive/being in charge for the purposes of prosecuting the relevant offence (*R (On the Application of Huntley)* v *DPP* [2004] EWHC 870 (Admin)).

The power of entry in connection with an offence under s. 4 is found in s. 17(1)(c)(iiia) of the Police and Criminal Evidence Act 1984 which states:

Subject to the following provisions of this section, and without prejudice to any other enactment, a constable may enter and search any premises for the purpose of arresting a person for an offence under

...

(iiia) section 4 (driving etc. when under influence of drink or drugs) or s. 163 (failure to stop when required to do so by constable in uniform) of the Road Traffic Act 1988.

The power of entry is only exercisable if the constable has reasonable grounds for believing that the person sought is on the premises (s. 17(2)(a)).

Under s. 4:

(3) ...a person shall be deemed not to have been in charge of a mechanically propelled vehicle if he proves that at the material time the circumstances were such that there was no likelihood of his driving it so long as he remained unfit to drive through drink or drugs.

KEYNOTE

This is only a defence to 'being in charge' of the vehicle while unfit; it is not a defence to 'driving' or 'attempting to drive' while unfit.

The onus is on the defendant to prove the fact that there was 'no likelihood' of driving. However, in determining whether the defendant was likely to drive the vehicle while unfit a court *may* disregard any injury to the defendant or damage to the vehicle (s. 4(4)).

The likelihood of driving is not an element of the offence itself; the intention of the defendant is material only to the statutory defence, which the defendant is required to prove on a balance of probabilities (*CPS* v *Bate* [2004] EWHC 2811 (Admin)).

3.5.2.1 Drugs

'Drugs' will include any intoxicant other than alcohol (s. 11); toluene found in some glues will amount to such a drug (*Bradford* v *Wilson* (1984) 78 Cr App R 77) as would insulin

(*Armstrong* v *Clark* [1957] 2 QB 391). In *R* v *Ealing Magistrates' Court, ex parte Woodman* [1994] RTR 189, the conviction of a diabetic suffering a hypoglycaemic attack was quashed because there was no evidence entitling the stipendiary magistrate to conclude that the presence of insulin in the applicant's blood was the real effective cause of the attack. The Divisional Court held that it would only be appropriate to rely on s. 4 in such cases where there is evidence of a clear overdose of insulin having been taken by the defendant.

3.5.2.2 Evidence of Impairment

A person shall be taken to be unfit to drive if his/her ability to drive properly is for the time being impaired (s. 4(5)).

Evidence of impairment is therefore essential and must be produced by the prosecution— this may be by expert opinion or by the evidence of a lay witness.

Impairment of ability to drive properly can be proved by evidence that a car was being driven erratically or had an accident at a spot where there was no hazard for a normal driver, provided, of course, that there is also evidence of drink or drugs. Opinion evidence of the defendant's state or the amount drunk by the defendant may be given by any 'lay' witness and does not require expert testimony, although such a witness cannot give evidence as to the defendant's ability to drive (*R* v *Lanfear* [1968] 2 QB 77). Witnesses who are not experts can give their general impression as to whether a person has had a drink (*R* v *Davies* [1962] 1 WLR 1111).

While it may be desirable (where unfitness to drive through drugs is at issue) that expert medical evidence is provided as to the defendant's degree of impairment, a lack of such evidence is not fatal to a prosecution. In *Leetham* v *DPP* [1999] RTR 29, the Divisional Court upheld a conviction under s. 4(1) based on the defendant's fast and erratic driving, his admitted consumption of cannabis, the presence of cannabis in his blood on subsequent analysis, the known effects of the drug and the evidence of the officers who stopped him that his eyes were red and glazed and that his speech was slow and slurred.

Evidence of impairment may be provided by the opinion evidence of an expert witness, normally a doctor, who has examined the defendant, even if the defendant has refused to be examined, and the expert's testimony should be treated as that of any 'independent expert witness giving evidence to assist the court', whether a police surgeon or anyone else (*Lanfear*).

It is not necessary to show what quantity of alcohol or drug the defendant had in his/her system for this offence. Therefore there is no need for any form of breath test although the prosecution may adduce evidence of the amount of alcohol or a drug in a specimen properly provided by the defendant under s. 7 of the Road Traffic Act 1988.

However, the police powers under s. 4 do not 'fall away' if you do embark on the procedure under s. 6 (e.g. requiring a breath sample: **see para. 3.5.4**). This was made clear in the decision of the Administrative Court in *DPP* v *Robertson* [2002] EWHC 542 (Admin). In that case, the officers had breathalysed the defendant who produced a negative result. However, on talking to the officers further, the defendant slurred his speech when giving the name of his solicitor. The officers then arrested the defendant under s. 4 (**see para. 3.5.2**) and took him to a police station where he provided an evidential sample of breath which was over the prescribed limit. The magistrates held that the defendant had been unlawfully arrested and the prosecutor appealed on a number of grounds. The Administrative Court held that it was quite conceivable to have a case where, notwithstanding that a driver had given a negative screening breath test, he/she was seen moments later staggering in a way that gave rise to a suspicion of unfitness. In such a case the law (s. 4) clearly gave a constable a power to arrest if what the constable had witnessed amounted to reasonable cause to suspect that the person was impaired.

3.5.3 Over Prescribed Limit

OFFENCE: **Driving or Attempting to Drive a Motor Vehicle while Over the Prescribed Limit—*Road Traffic Act 1988, s. 5(1)(a)***

> • Triable summarily • Six months' imprisonment and/or a fine • Obligatory disqualification

The Road Traffic Act 1988, s. 5 states:

> (1) If a person—
> (a) drives or attempts to drive a motor vehicle on a road or other public place,
> . . .
> after consuming so much alcohol that the proportion of it in his breath, blood or urine exceeds the prescribed limit he is guilty of an offence.

OFFENCE: **Being in Charge of a Motor Vehicle while Over the Prescribed Limit—*Road Traffic Act 1988, s. 5(1)(b)***

> • Triable summarily • Three months' imprisonment and/or a fine • Discretionary disqualification

The Road Traffic Act 1988, s. 5 states:

> (1) If a person—
> (a) . . .
> (b) is in charge of a motor vehicle on a road or other public place,
> after consuming so much alcohol that the proportion of it in his breath, blood or urine exceeds the prescribed limit he is guilty of an offence.

OFFENCE: **Driving or Attempting to Drive a Motor Vehicle with Concentration of Specified Controlled Drug above Specified Limit—*Road Traffic Act 1988, s. 5A(1)(a)***

> • Triable summarily • Six months' imprisonment and/or a fine • Obligatory disqualification

The Road Traffic Act 1988, s. 5A states:

> (1) This section applies where a person ('D')—
> (a) drives or attempts to drive a motor vehicle on a road or other public place, or
> . . .
> and there is in D's body a specified controlled drug.
> (2) D is guilty of an offence if the proportion of the drug in D's blood or urine exceeds the specified limit for that drug...

OFFENCE: **Being in Charge of a Motor Vehicle with Concentration of Specified Controlled Drug above Specified Limit—*Road Traffic Act 1988, s. 5A(1 (b)***

> • Triable summarily • Three months' imprisonment and/or a fine • Discretionary disqualification

The Road Traffic Act 1988, s. 5A states:

> (1) This section applies where a person ('D')—
> . . .
> (b) is in charge of a motor vehicle on a road or other public place,
> and there is in D's body a specified controlled drug.
> (2) D is guilty of an offence if the proportion of the drug in D's blood or urine exceeds the specified limit for that drug...

KEYNOTE

These offences apply to *motor vehicles* as defined in **chapter 3.1**.

Driving etc. Exceeding the Prescribed Limit—Alcohol

'Consuming' is not restricted to drinking and will encompass other methods of getting alcohol into the blood-stream (*DPP* v *Johnson* [1995] RTR 9).

The prescribed limit is:

- 35 microgrammes of alcohol in 100 millilitres of breath
- 80 milligrammes of alcohol in 100 millilitres of blood
- 107 milligrammes of alcohol in 100 millilitres of urine.

Section 11(2) which sets out these limits also allows for the levels to be changed.

The prosecution have to establish that the defendant's breath-alcohol content exceeded the permitted maximum; they do not have to establish a specific figure (*Gordon* v *Thorpe* [1986] RTR 358). The meaning of the word 'breath' in s. 5(1) of the 1988 Act is not confined to 'deep lung' air and should be given its dictionary definition of 'air exhaled from any thing' (*Zafar* v *DPP* [2004] EWHC 2468 (Admin)).

When dealing with the offence under s. 5(1)(b) it will be important to remember the statutory defence (**see para. 3.5.3.1**). The effect of this is that police officers investigating offences of being 'in charge' will have to ensure that a defendant is interviewed properly and fully as to all the circumstances, taking particular care to establish that the defendant is fully sober at the time of interview and establishing that there was a real risk of the defendant driving the vehicle while still over the prescribed limit.

The Divisional Court has held that there is some positive duty on a person to inquire whether a drink contains alcohol before drinking it if that person intends to drive afterwards (*Robinson* v *DPP* [2003] EWHC 2718 (Admin)).

The prescribed limits for drugs are inserted by the Drug Driving (Specified Limits) (England and Wales) Regulations 2014 (SI 2014/2868).

Driving etc. Exceeding the Specified Limit—Drugs

Drug	Limit (microgrammes per litre of blood)
Amphetamine	250
Benzoylecgonine	50
Clonazepam	50
Cocaine	10
Delta-9-Tetrahydrocannabinol	2
Diazepam	550
Flunitrazepam	300
Ketamine	20
Lorazepam	100
Lysergic Acid Diethylamide	1
Methadone	500
Methylamphetamine	10
Methylenedioxymethamphetamine	10
6-Monoacetylmorphine	5
Morphine	80
Oxazepam	300
Temazepam	1000

These are the limits described in s. 5A as 'specified limit for that drug'.

A device known as 'Drugwipe' is the first portable device that can detect the presence of cannabis (delta-9-tetrahydrocannabinol) and cocaine—two of the most common substances used by drug drivers. This would be the device that would be used when conducting a preliminary drug test (**see para. 3.5.4**).

3.5.3.1 Defences

The Road Traffic Act 1988, s. 5 states:

(2) It is a defence for a person charged with an offence under subsection (1)(b) above to prove that at the time he is alleged to have committed the offence the circumstances were such that there was no likelihood of his driving the vehicle whilst the proportion of alcohol in his breath, blood or urine remained likely to exceed the prescribed limit.

(3) The court may, in determining whether there was such a likelihood as is mentioned in subsection (2) above, disregard any injury to him and any damage to the vehicle.

The Road Traffic Act 1988, s. 5A states

(6) It is a defence for a person ('D') charged with an offence by virtue of subsection (1)(b) to prove that at the time D is alleged to have committed the offence the circumstances were such that there was no likelihood of D driving the vehicle whilst the proportion of the specified controlled drug in D's blood or urine remained likely to exceed the specified limit for that drug.

(7) The court may, in determining whether there was such a likelihood, disregard any injury to D and any damage to the vehicle.

KEYNOTE

This is effectively the same defence based around the likelihood of driving as it relates to driving whilst alcohol in breath, blood or urine remained likely to exceed the prescribed limit or whilst the proportion of a specified controlled drug in blood or urine remained likely to exceed the specified limit for that drug.

There is existing case law, decided at the time for alcohol only, but as the details relate to the essentials of 'likelihood of driving' this case law should be arguable in relation to the drug driving offence.

A good example of this defence in operation is the case of *CPS* v *Bate* [2004] EWHC 2811 (Admin). In that case the defendant had been found in a car with the keys to the ignition in his hand. Following a positive breath test, he appeared at court charged under s. 5(1)(b). The defendant argued that he had only been in the car for the purpose of retrieving a disabled permit before ringing his wife to arrange a taxi for him to get home. Although the magistrates' court accepted this account, the CPS argued that they were wrong to do so. The Divisional Court held that the magistrates had treated the likelihood of driving as an element of the offence itself. The court held that this was the wrong approach; that the defendant had manifestly been 'in charge' of the vehicle and had also been over the prescribed limit. Therefore the likelihood of the defendant's driving the vehicle while still over the limit was only relevant if and when he raised the statutory defence. If he chose to rely on that defence, the usual considerations with regard to standards of proof (set out below) would then apply.

The presence of a wheel clamp on a motor vehicle could not be discounted by the Divisional Court when considering the likelihood of the person being able to drive it while over the limit. The defendant had refused to pay the fee to have the wheel clamp on his car removed and while this did not constitute damage to the vehicle (as the clamp did not intrude on the integrity of the vehicle) the court held that there was no likelihood of his driving the vehicle (*Drake* v *DPP* [1994] Crim LR 855).

This defence was subjected to considerable scrutiny in a case where a defendant was found asleep in a van and, on being breathalysed, provided a reading that showed his alcohol to breath ratio to be four times the legal limit. The defendant claimed that there had been no likelihood of his driving while over the prescribed limit but the magistrates did not accept that he had proved the point sufficiently. The defendant then argued that the application of s. 5(2) was contrary to Article 6(2) of the European Convention on Human Rights (the presumption of innocence). Although the Divisional Court failed to agree at the first hearing and were still not unanimous on the second occasion, the majority decision was that the defence could be read as follows: 'It is a defence for a person charged with an offence under s. 5(1)(b) to *demonstrate from the evidence an arguable case that* at the time he is alleged to have committed the offence etc.' (emphasis added). Therefore, once the prosecution prove the elements of the offence beyond a reasonable doubt, the defendant must demonstrate an arguable case that there was no likelihood of his/her driving the vehicle while still over the prescribed limit. Once the defendant does this, the prosecution must then prove beyond a reasonable doubt that there *was* such a likelihood (*Sheldrake* v *DPP* [2003] EWHC 273 (Admin)). This case came before the House of Lords as

---

Attorney-General's Reference (No. 4 of 2002) (Sheldrake v *DPP)* [2004] UKHL 43. There it was held that, although the subsection did in fact infringe the presumption of innocence, the burden placed on the defendant was reasonable because it was in pursuance of a legitimate aim. The likelihood of the defendant's driving was a matter that was so closely linked to his/her own knowledge at the relevant time that it made it much more appropriate for the defendant to prove, on the balance of probabilities, that he/she would not have been likely to drive (as opposed to requiring the prosecution to prove the opposite, beyond a reasonable doubt).

The Road Traffic Act 1988, s. 5A states:

(3) It is a defence for a person ('D') charged with an offence under this section to show that—
  (a) the specified controlled drug had been prescribed or supplied to D for medical or dental purposes,
  (b) D took the drug in accordance with any directions given by the person by whom the drug was prescribed or supplied, and with any accompanying instructions (so far as consistent with any such directions) given by the manufacturer or distributor of the drug, and
  (c) D's possession of the drug immediately before taking it was not unlawful under section 5(1) of the Misuse of Drugs Act 1971 (restriction of possession of controlled drugs) because of an exemption in regulations made under section 7 of that Act (authorisation of activities otherwise unlawful under foregoing provisions)...
(4) The defence in subsection (3) is not available if D's actions were—
  (a) contrary to any advice, given by the person by whom the drug was prescribed or supplied, about the amount of time that should elapse between taking the drug and driving a motor vehicle, or
  (b) contrary to any accompanying instructions about that matter (so far as consistent with any such advice) given by the manufacturer or distributor of the drug.
(5) If evidence is adduced that is sufficient to raise an issue with respect to the defence in subsection (3), the court must assume that the defence is satisfied unless the prosecution proves beyond reasonable doubt that it is not...

KEYNOTE

This 'medical defence' will be available where:

- The drug was lawfully prescribed, supplied, or purchased over the counter, for medical or dental purposes; and
- The drug was taken in accordance with advice given by the person who prescribed or supplied the drug, and in accordance with any accompanying written instructions (so far as the latter are consistent with any advice of the prescriber).

The effect of s. 5A(4) is that prescribers and suppliers of medicines should give suitable clinical advice to patients regarding the time that should elapse after taking the drug supplied and before driving and drivers should be aware of any instructions provided with the medication in relation to this. Failing to adhere to this advice/instructions means the defence at s. 5A(3) is not available.

Once raised, the court will assume the defence is satisfied unless the prosecution proves that it is not to criminal standards.

3.5.4 Preliminary Tests

The relevant police powers now provide for three different types of preliminary test, set out under ss. 6A, 6B and 6C of the Road Traffic Act 1988.

The Road Traffic Act 1988, s. 6 states:

(1) If any of subsections (2) to (5) applies a constable may require a person to co-operate with any one or more preliminary tests administered to the person by that constable or another constable.

(2) This subsection applies if a constable reasonably suspects that the person—
    (a) is driving, is attempting to drive or is in charge of a motor vehicle on a road or other public place, and
    (b) has alcohol or a drug in his body or is under the influence of a drug.
(3) This subsection applies if a constable reasonably suspects that the person—
    (a) has been driving, attempting to drive or in charge of a motor vehicle on a road or other public place while having alcohol or a drug in his body or while unfit to drive because of a drug, and
    (b) still has alcohol or a drug in his body or is still under the influence of a drug.
(4) This subsection applies if a constable reasonably suspects that the person—
    (a) is or has been driving, attempting to drive or in charge of a motor vehicle on a road or other public place, and
    (b) has committed a traffic offence while the vehicle was in motion.

KEYNOTE

These powers allow the police to administer three preliminary tests: a breathalyser test, a test indicating whether a person is unfit to drive due to drink or drugs, and a test (a 'drug-wipe') to detect the presence of drugs in the person's body.

As s. 6(1) refers to 'any one or more preliminary tests' it is clear that they are not mutually exclusive and the constable could require co-operation with each of the tests in turn, if only to eliminate any suspicion in relation to alcohol or a drug.

The requirement must be made using words of sufficient clarity although there is no set format for any particular words to be uttered.

Although the police officer *making the requirement* does not have to be in uniform, the officer *administering* a preliminary test under s. 6(2)–(4) *must be in uniform* (s. 6(7)). This means that the officer administering the test must be in uniform whatever test is being administered (preliminary breath test, impairment test or drug test).

The circumstances fall into the three main categories set out at s. 6(2)–(4), with the final category (under s. 6(5)) relating to accidents (**see para. 3.5.4.3**). It can be seen from the categories above that they involve:

- the present—someone who is reasonably suspected to be driving, attempting to drive or being in charge of a motor vehicle on a road or other public place, and of having alcohol or a drug in his/her body or being under the influence of a drug;
- the past—someone reasonably suspected of having been driving, attempting to drive or in charge of a motor vehicle on a road or other public place while having alcohol or a drug in his/her body or while unfit to drive because of a drug, and who still has alcohol or a drug in his/her body or is still under the influence of a drug; and
- a combination of the past and present—someone who it is reasonably suspected is or has been driving, attempting to drive or in charge of a motor vehicle on a road or other public place, and who is reasonably suspected to have committed a traffic offence while the vehicle was in motion. 'Traffic offence' here means an offence under any provision of the Road Traffic Act 1988 (other than part V—driving instruction), the Road Traffic Offenders Act 1988, the Road Traffic Regulation Act 1984 and part II of the Public Passenger Vehicles Act 1981. Such offences, which include offences under any regulations made under those Acts, must have been committed while the vehicle was moving.

Random Tests

Although the police can use their powers to stop vehicles at random the law in England and Wales does not permit entirely random testing of drivers for drink or drugs (**see para. 3.2.2** for an explanation of this area of law).

3.5.4.1 'Reasonably Suspects'

There is a distinction between 'reasonably suspects' and 'reasonably believes' and whether the constable reasonably suspected or believed a fact in issue will be determined in the light of all the available evidence. The distinction between the two expressions has been held to be a significant one, intended by Parliament (*Baker* v *Oxford* [1980] RTR 315). In that case it was held that the deliberate use of the word 'believe' in the Act imposed a requirement for a greater degree of certainty in the mind of the officers concerned. While an officer might reasonably suspect someone has been drinking or taking drugs, a single error of judgement or carelessness on the part of a driver will not necessarily justify such a suspicion (see e.g. *Williams* v *Jones* [1972] RTR 4).

The importance of whether such suspicion or belief existed or not lies not only in triggering the relevant powers; it also has the potential to affect the nature of any conversation that might take place between the officer and a suspected driver. A good example of this can be seen in *R (On the Application of Ortega)* v *DPP* [2001] EWHC Admin 143. In that case the officers were held not to have had reasonable grounds to suspect that any offence had been committed at the time they questioned the defendant about his ownership and driving of a particular car. The absence of such reasonable grounds to suspect an offence meant that the doorstep conversation, which was not contemporaneously recorded and some of which took place without caution, was nevertheless admissible.

The important factor to consider when examining cases such as *Ortega* is that there is a huge difference between *reasonably suspecting that a person has alcohol or a drug in his/her body or is under the influence of a drug* and *reasonably suspecting a person of committing an offence*—they are not the same thing. Reasonably suspecting that someone has alcohol/drug in his/her body does not trigger a requirement to caution a person before speaking to him/her in such circumstances. The reasonable suspicion in relation to the alcohol/drug may trigger the power to require a person to take part in a preliminary test. The result of that preliminary test, e.g. by providing a positive breath test, may then, in turn, provide the reasonable suspicion that the person has committed an offence and this suspicion triggers the need to caution along with other powers (such as the power of arrest and/or a power of entry). The screening test is indicative only and is only relevant as to whether a constable should arrest the suspect with a view to securing an evidential specimen thereafter.

With the above in mind, you can now understand why the Divisional Court has held that a 'roadside confession' before any caution was given is admissible where it was made prior to the driver being given a breath test (*Whelehan* v *DPP* [1995] RTR 177). In that case the defendant was found sitting in the driver's seat of a car at the roadside with the keys in the ignition. On being approached by a police officer, he admitted that he had been drinking and was then asked if he had driven to that location. The driver replied that he had and was required to provide a roadside screening breath test which was positive. The driver was convicted of driving while over the prescribed limit. Dismissing his appeal, the court held that the time, place and circumstances in which he had been found afforded sufficient evidence to infer that he had driven to the scene, quite apart from the admission. The magistrates' court had been entitled to find that it was only *after* the roadside breath test that the police officer suspected an offence had been committed and therefore it was only then the need to caution arose. This is exactly the situation described above—reasonable suspicion regarding the presence of alcohol/drug is not reasonable suspicion that someone has committed an offence.

Of course, if officers do reasonably suspect that someone has committed an offence in relation to drink/drive matters they should caution the suspect as they would do in any other circumstances.

In addition to first-hand observation of a driver's behaviour, reasonable suspicion may arise from the observations of another officer (*Erskine* v *Hollin* [1971] RTR 199) and this is clearly provided for now in the extended wording of s. 6. Reasonable suspicion may even arise from information provided by a member of the public (*DPP* v *Wilson* [1991] RTR 284). An officer receiving a radio message that a driver had been seen driving erratically may thereby acquire enough reasonable suspicion to require the administering of one of the three preliminary tests on that basis.

3.5.4.2 The Tests

The Road Traffic Act 1988 states:

6A Preliminary breath test

(1) A preliminary breath test is a procedure whereby the person to whom the test is administered provides a specimen of breath to be used for the purpose of obtaining, by means of a device of a type approved by the Secretary of State, an indication whether the proportion of alcohol in the person's breath or blood is likely to exceed the prescribed limit.

(2) A preliminary breath test administered in reliance on section 6(2) to (4) may be administered only at or near the place where the requirement to co-operate with the test is imposed.

6B Preliminary impairment test

(1) A preliminary impairment test is a procedure whereby the constable administering the test—

(a) observes the person to whom the test is administered in his performance of tasks specified by the constable, and

(b) makes such other observations of the person's physical state as the constable **thinks** expedient.

…

(4) A preliminary impairment test may be administered—

(a) at or near the place where the requirement to co-operate with the test is imposed, or

(b) if the constable who imposes the requirement thinks it expedient, at a police station specified by him.

6C Preliminary drug test

(1) A preliminary drug test is a procedure by which a specimen of sweat or saliva is—

(a) obtained, and

(b) used for the purpose of obtaining, by means of a device of a type approved by the Secretary of State, an indication whether the person to whom the test is administered has a drug in his body and if so—

(i) whether it is a specified controlled drug;

(ii) if it is, whether the proportion of it in the person's blood or urine is likely to exceed the specified limit for that drug.

(2) A preliminary drug test may be administered—

(a) at or near the place where the requirement to co-operate with the test is imposed, or

(b) if the constable who imposes the requirement thinks it expedient, at a police station specified by him.

(3) Up to three preliminary drug tests may be administered.

KEYNOTE

The officer administering any of the tests above must be in uniform (s. 6(7)) (see para. 3.2.2). This uniform requirement does not apply in the case of preliminary tests following an accident (as to which see para. 3.5.4.3).

The tests referred to at ss. 6A and 6C are for the purpose of obtaining, by means of a device of a type approved by the Secretary of State, an indication whether the proportion of either alcohol or drugs in a person's breath or blood is likely to exceed the prescribed limit as it relates to alcohol or the specific drug. This is an important distinction as the preliminary test is undertaken only to give an indication to the officer administering it of the likelihood of the offence, not for proving the relevant offence. This is evident from the fact that the prosecution are not obliged to disclose to the defence the results in figures from a roadside test (*Smith* v *DPP* [2007] 4 All ER 1135).

Failure to comply with the manufacturer's instructions on the use of approved devices has always raised contentious points and will no doubt continue to do so. Generally, failing to follow key instructions of the manufacturer such as assembling the tube on a breathalyser or allowing the driver to smoke immediately before taking the test, has meant that the person has not provided a preliminary test and he/she may be asked to provide another; refusing to do so will be an offence (see para. 3.5.4.4) (*DPP* v *Carey* [1970] AC 1072). The Divisional Court also decided that an innocent failure by a police officer to follow the manufacturer's instructions should not be deemed to render either the test or any subsequent arrest unlawful (*DPP* v *Kay* [1999] RTR 109).

Note that the legislation for preliminary breath tests prevents drivers from claiming an extra 20 minutes' grace by pretending that they have just had a drink (*Grant* v *DPP* [2003] EWHC 130 (Admin)). Similar efforts to manipulate the circumstances in light of the relevant manufacturer's instructions for the other tests can be expected to receive similar treatment from the courts.

A preliminary breath test under s. 6A may only be administered at or near the place where the requirement to co-operate with the test is imposed unless it is made under the provisions relating to accidents (see para. 3.5.4.3). The other two tests, under ss. 6B and 6C, may be administered at or near the place where the requirement to co-operate is imposed, or if the constable imposing it thinks it expedient, at a police station specified by the constable. A preliminary impairment test under s. 6B is a completely different procedure from the other two and involves an appropriately trained police officer authorised by his/her chief officer observing the person performing specified tasks and that officer making such other observations of the person's physical state as he/she thinks 'expedient'. The types of tests are set out in a Code of Practice published by the Secretary of State and include pupillary examination, walk-and-turn tests and finger-to-nose tests. The police officer administering a preliminary impairment test must have regard to the Code of Practice (s. 6B(5)) and can only administer such a test if approved for that purpose by his/her chief officer (s. 6B(6)).

The preliminary drug test under s. 6C is introduced to enable officers to carry out a roadside test that detects drugs in the driver's body and up to three preliminary drug tests may be administered to ascertain whether the person has a specified controlled drug in his/her body and, if so, whether it is likely that it exceeds the specified limit.

3.5.4.3 Procedure Following an Accident

The Road Traffic Act 1988, s. 6 states:

(5) This subsection applies if—
   (a) an accident occurs owing to the presence of a motor vehicle on a road or other public place, and
   (b) a constable reasonably believes that the person was driving, attempting to drive or in charge of the vehicle at the time of the accident.

KEYNOTE

In relying on this section you must show that an accident had 'occurred', i.e. it has in fact taken place, not simply that you suspected or even believed that to be the case (*Chief Constable of West Midlands Police* v *Billingham* [1979] RTR 446). It is important to emphasise that the meaning is not restricted to that given to a 'reportable' accident under s. 170 (see para. 3.4.1).

The requirement here is for the officer to have a 'reasonable belief' that the person was driving, attempting to drive or in charge of a relevant vehicle at the time of an accident (for 'reasonable belief' see para. 3.5.4.1).

There is no need for the police officer making the requirement to believe or even suspect that the person has been drinking, or that he/she has committed any offence; reasonable belief in his/her involvement (as a person driving, attempting to drive or being in charge of a vehicle) in the accident is enough. *Nor is there a need for the officer making the requirement or administering the preliminary test to be in uniform.*

A preliminary *breath test* (under s. 6A) administered under the above provisions may be administered:

(a) at or near the place where the requirement to co-operate with the test is imposed, or
(b) if the constable who imposes the requirement thinks it expedient, at a police station specified by the constable (s. 6A(3)).

Note that there is no general power of entry in order to administer preliminary breath tests, however there is a specific power of entry in relation to the above subsection (see para. 3.5.4.6).

Where an officer has imposed a requirement to co-operate with a preliminary breath test in circumstances where s. 6(5) applies, he/she may also require an evidential breath specimen under s. 7 (as to which see para. 3.5.5.1) at or near the place where the preliminary breath test has been administered or would have been but for the person's failure to co-operate.

Where a constable imposes a requirement to co-operate with a preliminary breath test at any place, he/she is entitled to remain at or near that place in order to impose on the person a requirement for an evidential specimen under s. 7 (s. 7(2C)) there.

3.5.4.4 Failure to Co-operate with Preliminary Test

OFFENCE: **Failing to Co-operate with a Preliminary Test—*Road Traffic Act 1988, s. 6(6)***

- Triable summarily • Fine • Discretionary disqualification

The Road Traffic Act 1988, s. 6 states:

(6) A person commits an offence if without reasonable excuse he fails to co-operate with a preliminary test in pursuance of a requirement imposed under this section.

KEYNOTE

As with any requirement carrying a sanction for failure to comply, you must show that the requirement for the preliminary test was properly made in accordance with the relevant conditions set out earlier in this paragraph. It will also need to be shown that the person both heard and understood the requirement.

An example of 'reasonable excuse' would be where the defendant is physically unable to co-operate with the requirement or where to do so would entail a substantial risk to the defendant's health (see e.g. *R* v *Lennard* [1973] 1 WLR 483).

Failing includes a refusal (s. 11(2)).

A person does not co-operate with a preliminary test or provide a specimen of breath for analysis unless his/her co-operation or the specimen:

(a) is sufficient to allow the test or the analysis to be carried out, and
(b) is provided in such a way as to enable the objective of the test or analysis to be satisfactorily achieved (s. 11(3)).

Therefore, if the person does not follow the instructions given or does something which purports to fulfil the requirement made by the officer but which does not meet the criteria in s. 11(3), he/she has 'failed' to co-operate. However, it is not necessary for the officer to produce a breath test device before this offence can be committed. The person's attitude and conduct after being required to give a breath specimen under s. 6A may be sufficient to make out the offence above and the evidence of the officer witnessing this attitude or conduct may suffice as proof that it amounted to a failure or refusal. In the event that a person clearly does something which amounts to a refusal to provide a preliminary breath test, the offence will be made out even though the officer did not produce a device for doing so (*DPP* v *Swan* [2004] EWHC 2432 (Admin)).

Having been required to provide a specimen of breath, a person may also be required to wait until a device is brought to the scene; failing to wait for a reasonable time, or doing anything which demonstrates an intention not to provide the specimen can amount to a 'failure' (*R* v *Wagner* [1970] Crim LR 535).

Simply producing enough breath to enable the device to give a positive reading does not necessarily mean the defendant has 'provided a specimen'; he/she must produce sufficient breath in the manner required to enable the device to give a reliable reading—positive or negative (*DPP* v *Heywood* [1998] RTR 1).

3.5.4.5 Powers of Arrest

The Road Traffic Act 1988, s. 6D states:

(1) A constable may arrest a person without warrant if as a result of a preliminary breath test or preliminary drug test the constable reasonably suspects that—
   (a) the proportion of alcohol in the person's breath or blood exceeds the prescribed limit, or
   (b) the person has a specified controlled drug in his body and the proportion of it in the person's blood or urine exceeds the specified limit for that drug.

(1A) ...

(2) A constable may arrest a person without warrant if—
   (a) the person fails to co-operate with a preliminary test in pursuance of a requirement imposed under section 6, and
   (b) the constable reasonably suspects that the person has alcohol or a drug in his body or is under the influence of a drug.

(2A) A person arrested under this section may, instead of being taken to a police station, be detained at or near the place where the preliminary test was, or would have been, administered, with a view to imposing on him there a requirement under section 7 of this Act.

(3) A person may not be arrested under this section while at a hospital as a patient.

KEYNOTE

The power of arrest is divided into two parts, neither of which requires the officer to be in uniform.

The first part relates to the situation where an officer (not necessarily the arresting officer) has administered a preliminary breath test under s. 6A or a preliminary drug test under s. 6C. If any officer reasonably suspects, as a result of that preliminary test, that the proportion of alcohol in the person's breath or blood exceeds the prescribed limit or a specified controlled drug in the person's blood or urine exceeds the specified limit for that drug, the officer may arrest the person without warrant. However, there is no obligation to do so.

Note that even where evidential specimens have been provided under s. 7 this does not prevent the power of arrest under s. 6D(1) from having effect (see para. 3.5.5.1).

The second part of the section allows any officer to arrest a person who fails to co-operate with any preliminary test imposed under s. 6 provided the officer reasonably suspects that the person has alcohol or a drug in his/her body or is under the influence of a drug. Without this reasonable suspicion, s. 6D(2) provides no power of arrest for failing to co-operate with a preliminary test.

Instead of being taken to a police station, a person who is arrested under this section may be detained at or near the place where the preliminary test was, or would have been, administered, with a view to imposing a requirement for an evidential specimen under s. 7 there.

3.5.4.6 Powers of Entry

There is a specific power of entry provided by the Road Traffic Act 1988, s. 6E as follows:

(1) A constable may enter any place (using reasonable force if necessary) for the purpose of—
   (a) imposing a requirement by virtue of section 6(5) following an accident in a case where the constable reasonably suspects that the accident involved injury of any person, or
   (b) arresting a person under section 6D following an accident in a case where the constable reasonably suspects that the accident involved injury of any person.

KEYNOTE

The wording of this subsection limits the purposes of entry to:

- Imposing a requirement for a preliminary test after an accident (s. 6(5)). To enter you must *know* there has been an accident, *suspect* that accident involved an injury to any person and *believe* that the person was driving/attempting to drive/in charge at the time of the accident.
- Arresting the person if, as a result of a preliminary breath test, the officer reasonably suspects that the proportion of alcohol in the person's breath or blood exceeds the prescribed limit; (arrest under s. 6D(1)). To enter you must *know* there has been an accident, *suspect* that the accident involved an injury to any person and *suspect* that the proportion of alcohol in the person's breath or blood exceeds the prescribed limit.
- Arresting the person for failing to co-operate with a preliminary test where the officer reasonably suspects that the person has alcohol or a drug in his/her body or is under the influence of a drug (arrest under s. 6D(2)). To enter you must *know* there has been an accident, *suspect* that the accident involved an injury to any person (the person must have failed to co-operate with any preliminary test) and you must *suspect* that the person has alcohol or a drug in his/her body or is under the influence of a drug.

3.5.4.7 Trespassing

Many legal arguments have raged over the legitimacy of a breath test carried out or requested where the officers concerned are in fact trespassing on the property of another. The results of these deliberations are:

- If police officers are trespassing *on the defendant's property* they are not entitled to require a breath test (*R* v *Fox* [1986] AC 281).
- If the officers are trespassing at the time they make the requirement, any subsequent arrest made by them is unlawful (*Clowser* v *Chaplin* [1981] RTR 317).
- Although the entry and the arrest may be unlawful, this will only affect the offence under s. 6(4) and not any other offences detected at the police station.
- Any requirement for a sample of breath properly made, and any subsequent arrest remains lawful *until* the officers become trespassers. A police officer, like any other member of the public, has an implied licence to go onto certain parts of someone's property (e.g. the front doorstep) unless and until that licence is withdrawn. If police officers go onto such a part of the defendant's property, they are not trespassing until told to leave and any requirement for a breath test, or any arrest made before this happens will be lawful. (See *Pamplin* v *Fraser* [1981] RTR 494 where the defendant drove onto his own land and locked himself in his car. It was held that the officers' licence to enter the land had not been withdrawn at that stage.) Telling officers to 'fuck off' is not necessarily enough to withdraw this implied licence (*Snook* v *Mannion* [1982] RTR 321).
- A person cannot seek refuge on someone else's land as a trespasser; a requirement for a breath test and any subsequent arrest may be lawful if the person is a trespasser (*Morris* v *Beardmore* [1980] RTR 321).
- If a person has been lawfully arrested on his/her own land, officers may remain on the land and enter premises to recapture that person, even if asked to leave (*Hart* v *Chief Constable of Kent* [1983] Crim LR 117).
- Although the provisions of s. 15(2) of the Road Traffic Offenders Act 1988 may render evidence from a specimen taken after an unlawful arrest admissible, any finding that the officer(s) concerned acted in a way that they knew to be unlawful or unwarranted may lead to that evidence being excluded under s. 78 of the Police and Criminal Evidence Act 1984 (*DPP* v *Godwin* [1991] RTR 303).

3.5.5   Evidential Specimens

Sections 7 to 9 of the Road Traffic Act 1988 govern the procedure for obtaining specimens for analysis, or evidential specimens. Unlike the preliminary breath tests above, specimens taken under this part of the Act are retained for evidential purposes in subsequent hearings. Such specimens will either be by breath samples taken on an approved machine (e.g. the Lion Intoximeter or the Camic Breath Analyser) or by blood/urine samples.

Minor errors in the printing functions of such machines will not necessarily invalidate the evidence produced by the machine, provided it can be shown that the analytical function of the machine was calibrated and working properly (*Reid* v *DPP* [1999] RTR 357).

Many of the difficulties which have been encountered during the police station process have now been addressed by police forces adopting a national pro-forma and strict adherence to those forms will significantly reduce the likelihood of convictions being quashed.

3.5.5.1   Provision of Specimens for Analysis

The Road Traffic Act 1988, s. 7 states:

(1) In the course of an investigation into whether a person has committed an offence under section 3A, 4 or 5 of this Act a constable may, subject to the following provisions of this section and section 9 of this Act, require him—
   (a) to provide two specimens of breath for analysis by means of a device of a type approved by the Secretary of State, or
   (b) to provide a specimen of blood or urine for a laboratory test.

(1A)   In the course of an investigation into whether a person has committed an offence under section 5A of this Act a constable may, subject to subsections (3) to (7) of this section and section 9 of this Act, require the person to provide a specimen of blood or urine for a laboratory test.

(2)   A constable may make a requirement under this section to provide specimens of breath only if—

(a)   the requirement is made at a police station or a hospital,

(b)   the requirement is imposed in circumstances where section 6(5) of this Act applies, or

(c)   the constable is in uniform.

...

(2C)   Where a constable has imposed a requirement on the person concerned to co-operate with a relevant breath test at any place, he is entitled to remain at or near that place in order to impose on him there a requirement under this section.

(2CA)   For the purposes of subsection (2C) 'a relevant breath test' is a procedure involving the provision by the person concerned of a specimen of breath to be used for the purpose of obtaining an indication whether the proportion of alcohol in his breath or blood is likely to exceed the prescribed limit.

(2D)   If a requirement under subsection (1)(a) above has been made at a place other than at a police station, such a requirement may subsequently be made at a police station if (but only if)—

(a)   a device or a reliable device of the type mentioned in subsection (1)(a) above was not available at that place or it was for any other reason not practicable to use such a device there, or

(b)   the constable who made the previous requirement has reasonable cause to believe that the device used there has not produced a reliable indication of the proportion of alcohol in the breath of the person concerned.

(3)   A requirement under this section to provide a specimen of blood or urine can only be made at a police station or at a hospital; and it cannot be made at a police station unless—

(a)   the constable making the requirement has reasonable cause to believe that for medical reasons a specimen of breath cannot be provided or should not be required, or

(b)   specimens of breath have not been provided elsewhere and at the time the requirement is made a device or a reliable device of the type mentioned in subsection (1)(a) above is not available at the police station or it is then for any other reason not practicable to use such a device there, or

(bb)   a device of the type mentioned in subsection (1)(a) above has been used (at the police station or elsewhere) but the constable who required the specimens of breath has reasonable cause to believe that the device has not produced a reliable indication of the proportion of alcohol in the breath of the person concerned, or

(bc)   as a result of the administration of a preliminary drug test, the constable making the requirement has reasonable cause to believe that the person required to provide a specimen of blood or urine has a drug in his body, or

(c)   the suspected offence is one under section 3A, 4 or 5A of this Act and the constable making the requirement has been advised by a medical practitioner or a registered health care professional that the condition of the person required to provide the specimen might be due to some drug;

but may then be made notwithstanding that the person required to provide the specimen has already provided or been required to provide two specimens of breath.

(4)   ...

(5)   A specimen of urine shall be provided within one hour of the requirement for its provision being made and after the provision of a previous specimen of urine.

(5A)   A constable may arrest a person without warrant if—

(a)   the person fails to provide a specimen of breath when required to do so in pursuance of this section, and

(b)   the constable reasonably suspects that the person has alcohol in his body.

(6)   A person who, without reasonable excuse, fails to provide a specimen when required to do so in pursuance of this section is guilty of an offence.

(7)   A constable must, on requiring any person to provide a specimen in pursuance of this section, warn him that a failure to provide it may render him liable to prosecution.

KEYNOTE

As well as taking evidential breath samples at the police station a police officer can now proceed directly to an evidential breath test at the roadside if in possession of a portable evidential device, without the need to carry out a preliminary test and arrest the person if they fail to provide such a sample (s. 5A).

As the evidential samples taken will form part of the case against a defendant, a lot of attention is paid to the device that was used and the extent to which its readings can be relied upon, as well as the due process to obtain such samples. To assist with this a series of MG DD forms are used to assist the police officer in following due procedure. In *Afolayan* v *CPS* [2012] EWHC 1322 (Admin), although Form MG DD/A had not been properly completed, the Divisional Court concluded that the justices had evidence from the police and from what the analyst said about the specimen she received entitling them to prefer that evidence to the defendant's evidence that the blood sample taken from him had not been sealed, as required, in his presence.

There are detailed guidelines available to operators conducting evidential tests to ensure the reliability of the results produced. Just as a failure to follow the key requirements by the *defendant* can amount to a failure/refusal to provide, similarly a failure by the *operator* to follow such a requirement can allow the procedure to be challenged. However, in the latter case any failure must be such as to affect the *reliability* of the test. It is common for device manufacturers to issue guidelines that require a 20-minute period free from consumption of alcohol or other substances prior to the administration of the test. In *DPP* v *Carey* [1970] AC 1072, the House of Lords ruled that if an officer has no knowledge or reason to suspect consumption of any substances within the relevant 20-minute period, the test remains valid even if it later transpires that some substance was actually consumed during that 20-minute period. If the officer *does* have knowledge or reason to suspect such consumption, then 20 minutes should be allowed to elapse before administering the test. In *Coulter* v *DPP* [2005] EWHC 1533 (Admin) the defendant had provided a positive breath specimen during a roadside screening test. During the police station procedure to obtain an evidential specimen the police officer asked if he had eaten anything. The defendant said he might have had a 'tic-tac' sweet. The officer nevertheless continued with the procedure and required a specimen of breath. The defendant refused and was charged under s. 7(6) of the Road Traffic Act 1988 (and the Road Traffic Offenders Act 1988, sch. 2). The police officer had been unaware of the guidelines recommending a 20-minute wait before testing a driver who had eaten recently before continuing with the procedure. The magistrates' court held that there was no case to answer as the officer should have waited 20 minutes before requiring a breath specimen and because the officer had been unable to show that the waiting period was not mandatory. On appeal by the DPP, the Divisional Court held that there was nothing in s. 7 to indicate that a requirement to produce a breath specimen was unlawful if the particular police guidelines were not followed. While it is possible for a failure to follow the guidelines to affect the reliability of a specimen, the court held that was not relevant in the instant case as no specimen of breath was ever provided.

While the reliability of a reading made by any device in any particular case is always open to challenge by way of admissible evidence, a defendant does not have an automatic right to challenge the Secretary of State's approval of devices every time they are used (*DPP* v *Memery* [2002] EWHC 1720 (Admin)).

In the case of a breath specimen it is presumed that the machine used was reliable; if that presumption is challenged by relevant evidence, the magistrates will have to be satisfied that the machine had provided a reading on which they could rely before they make the assumption (*DPP* v *Brown and Teixeira* [2001] EWHC 931 (Admin); *Cracknell* v *Willis* [1988] AC 450). This rebuttable presumption was tested by a well-known rugby player who argued on the grounds of only drinking an expresso martini that the machine was not reliable. The senior District Judge at Westminster Magistrates' Court disagreed and supported the decision in *Cracknell*. In *R (On the Application of Hassani)* v *West London Magistrates' Court* [2017] EWHC 1270 (Admin) the court affirmed and restated the decision of the Chief Magistrate and Senior District Judge in *CPS* v *Cipriani* [2016] giving extensive guidance in relation to the conduct of drink drive cases including case management at the first hearing, disclosure, expert witnesses and challenging the reliability of breath machines.

Where there are reasons to believe that a type of device is generally unreliable (as opposed to the specific device used in a particular case), representations should be made to the Secretary of State (*R* v *Skegness Magistrates' Court, ex parte Cardy* [1985] RTR 49); it is not open to magistrates to consider whether the type of device should be on the list of 'approved devices' because of some alleged general design flaw (*DPP* v *Brown and Teixeira*).

The Queen's Bench Division examined two cases where the machine gave an 'ambient fail' yet went on to give a further, fresh sample that was positive. In the first case the court held the sample was reliable despite the 'ambient fail' and allowed the roadside result to support the positive reading. In the second case the appeal was allowed, however this appears to be more linked to the drafting of the questions by the examining magistrate and the inconsistencies of the officers' evidence than the reliability of the machine. It seems the courts are unwilling to allow technical defences but remain strong on the actual procedure carried out (*DPP* v *Vince* [2016] EWHC 3014 (Admin)).

The fact that specimens of breath have been provided under s. 7 does not prevent the power of arrest (under s. 6D(1)—see para. 3.5.4.6) having effect if the constable who imposed the requirement to provide the specimens has reasonable cause to believe that the device used to analyse the specimens has not produced a reliable indication of the proportion of alcohol in the breath of the person (s. 6D(1A)).

Urine samples do not need to be taken by a medical practitioner. The samples will be admissible as long as they are provided within the time set out under s. 7(5) and there are two distinct samples (as opposed to two samples taken during the same act of urinating) (*Prosser* v *Dickeson* [1982] RTR 96). In *Ryder* v *CPS* [2011] EWHC 4003 (Admin) the Administrative Court held that obtaining the urine sample from a catheterised patient amounted to more than one sample. The court held that if someone had to drain their urine into a catheter, and this was treated as a single sample, the person on a catheter would never be able to supply a specimen of urine for analysis. This would usurp due process. This conclusion is consistent with the guidance offered by May LJ in *Nugent* v *Ridley* [1987] RTR 412 that the specimen to be analysed must be 'a fresh specimen and properly reflects the bodily condition of the person from whom it is taken'.

The hour within which the specimens must be produced starts from the time the request is made. However, the defendant must be given the opportunity to provide the urine within the one-hour period (*Robertson* v *DPP* [2004] EWHC 517 (Admin)).

It would appear by the wording of s. 7(3)(bc) and (c) that where a preliminary drug test has been carried out the officer can require a specimen of blood/urine without the advice of a medical practitioner or a registered health care professional. However in ss. 3, 4 or 5A offences where a preliminary drug test has not been carried out the advice of a medical practitioner or a registered health care professional must be sought before the power to request blood/urine can be made. When such medical advice is sought, the doctor or a registered health care professional must give the officer a clear verbal statement to the effect that the driver's condition was due to some drug before the power arises (*Cole* v *DPP* [1988] RTR 224); however the doctor is not limited to the findings of his own examination at the police station, but is entitled to take into account all relevant information, including what he has been told by police officers (*Angel* v *Chief Constable of South Yorkshire* [2010] EWHC 883 (Admin)).

3.5.5.2 The Requirement

Unlike the requirement for specimens of blood or urine, a requirement under s. 7 to provide evidential *breath* specimens can be made:

(a) at a police station,

(b) at a hospital, or

(c) at or near a place where a preliminary breath test has been administered to that person or would have been but for his/her failure to co-operate with it.

That requirement can be made of more than one person in respect of the same vehicle (e.g. if it is believed that one of three defendants was driving the vehicle) (*Pearson* v *Metropolitan Police Commissioner* [1988] RTR 276). A requirement under s. 7 to provide specimens of breath cannot be made at or near the place where a preliminary breath test has been administered to the person (or would have been but for his/her failure to co-operate) unless the constable making it:

• is in uniform, or

• has imposed a requirement on the person concerned to co-operate with a preliminary breath test in circumstances where s. 6(5) applies (i.e. following an accident).

Note that where a constable has imposed a requirement on the person concerned to co-operate with a preliminary breath test at any place, the constable is entitled to remain at or near that place in order to impose on the person a requirement for an evidential specimen under s. 7 there (s. 7(2C)).

If a requirement for an evidential breath specimen is made under s. 7(1)(a) at a place other than at a police station, such a requirement can still be made later *at* a police station but only if:

- a device or a reliable device was not available at that place or it was for any other reason not practicable to use such a device there, or
- the constable who made the previous requirement has reasonable cause to believe that the device used there has not produced a reliable indication of the proportion of alcohol in the breath of the person concerned (s. 7(2D)).

A requirement for blood or urine can be made at a police station or hospital if the conditions under s. 7(3)(a)–(c) are met.

3.5.5.3 Medical Reasons

For the officer making the requirement to have 'reasonable cause to *believe*' that medical reasons exist, there is no need to seek medical advice first (*Dempsey* v *Catton* [1986] RTR 194). It is the objective *cause* of that belief which will be considered by the courts, not whether the officer actually did believe that a medical reason existed (*Davis* v *DPP* [1988] RTR 156). This was demonstrated in *Bodhaniya* v *CPS* [2013] EWHC 1743 (Admin) where the officer made this requirement after five failed attempts by the defendant to provide an evidential breath sample. The defendant appealed the conviction, stating that the request for blood was unlawful. The officer contended that by failing to provide an evidential breath sample five times the only reasonable inference was that there had been a medical reason for the defendant not doing so; the appeal was dismissed.

In *Kinsella* v *DPP* [2002] EWHC 545 (QB), the Divisional Court held that, just because the defendant had a mouth spray (for angina) and tablets at the time of arrest, that did not of itself impose an obligation on the relevant police officer to consult a doctor before deciding that any specimen to be provided would be blood. In that case the officer had asked the defendant if there were any medical reasons why blood should not be taken and he had said that there were not.

Where an officer specifically asks whether there are any medical reasons for not taking a blood sample, the officer is entitled to rely on the answer given unless it is obvious that such reasons exist (*Jubb* v *DPP* [2002] EWHC 2317 (Admin)).

If a person is too drunk to provide a breath specimen, that may be regarded as a 'medical' reason for requiring a sample of blood/urine (*Young* v *DPP* [1992] RTR 328).

3.5.5.4 Device 'Available'?

If the relevant machine at a police station will not calibrate or is in some other way unreliable, this would appear to make it 'unavailable'. In such a case, however, the driver may be taken to another police station where such a machine is 'available'; this may be done *even if the driver has already provided two samples on the inaccurate machine* (*Denny* v *DPP* [1990] RTR 417).

Whether a machine is 'available' if it produces an accurate reading of the analysis of the driver's breath but cannot, for some reason, produce a hard copy printout of that reading is open to some doubt. In one case (*Morgan* v *Lee* [1985] RTR 409) where the officer did not know of the machine's defect, his subsequent request for a blood sample was held to have been unlawful. However, in a later case the Divisional Court held that, if the officer knew at the time that the machine had any form of malfunction, he/she could require a specimen of blood/urine under s. 7(3)(b) (*Thompson* v *Thynne* [1986] Crim LR 629) and this *subjective* approach has been followed and approved many times since.

Where the requirement for blood/urine is made under s. 7(3)(b), that sample must be used and the prosecution cannot revert to evidence produced by the breath sample (*Badkin* v *Chief Constable of South Yorkshire* [1988] RTR 401).

If the option to provide a blood sample is chosen, then, again, the driver may be taken to another police station where a doctor is available (*Chief Constable of Kent v Berry* [1986] Crim LR 748).

Section 7(3)(b) also allows the officer (**see para. 3.5.5.1**) the option of a blood/urine specimen when, 'for any other reason' it is not practicable to use a breath-testing device at the police station. This would clearly include the situation where no trained operator is available to work the machine (*Chief Constable of Avon and Somerset v Kelliher* [1986] Crim LR 635).

3.5.5.5 Warning

The warning required by s. 7(7) is critical to a successful prosecution for failing to provide a specimen when required under s. 7(3). It is not needed when a driver elects to give an alternative sample under s. 8 (**see para. 3.5.5.10**) (see *Hayes v DPP* [1993] Crim LR 966 and also *DPP v Jackson; Stanley v DPP* [1999] 1 AC 406 at **para. 3.5.5.6, Keynote**).

3.5.5.6 Choice by Officer

The Road Traffic Act 1988, s. 7 states:

(4) If the provision of a specimen other than a specimen of breath may be required in pursuance of this section the question whether it is to be a specimen of blood or a specimen of urine and, in the case of a specimen of blood, the question who is to be asked to take it shall be decided (subject to subsection (4A)) by the constable making the requirement.

(4A) Where a constable decides for the purposes of subsection (4) to require the provision of a specimen of blood, there shall be no requirement to provide such a specimen if—
  (a) the medical practitioner who is asked to take the specimen is of the opinion that, for medical reasons, it cannot or should not be taken; or
  (b) the registered health care professional who is asked to take it is of that opinion and there is no contrary opinion from a medical practitioner;
  and, where by virtue of this subsection there can be no requirement to provide a specimen of blood, the constable may require a specimen of urine instead.

KEYNOTE

In exercising the power under s. 7(3), the decision as to whether the specimen will be blood or urine will be made *by the officer*.

In *DPP v Warren* [1993] AC 319 the House of Lords stated unequivocally that the decision, in both situations, is to be made by the officer. However, that is not to say that the officer can simply assume that blood should be taken unless medical reasons prevent it, nor that the officer should take no notice of any information given by the driver. The statutory discretion given to the officer by s. 7(4), although wide, has to be exercised reasonably (*Joseph v DPP* [2003] EWHC 3078 (Admin)). In *Joseph* the driver told the officer that he was a Rastafarian and therefore could not give blood. The officer's insistence that the driver give blood anyway, even though there was no reason not to take urine instead, was held to be so unreasonable as to make it unlawful.

Following the decision in *Warren*, many forces adapted their pro-formas in order to close what Lord Bridge called *a variety of wholly unmeritorious avenues of escape from conviction*. This has not stopped cases being argued in relation to choice and when it must be given to a defendant when explaining the choices available under s. 7(4).

In *Fraser v DPP* [1997] RTR 373, Lord Bingham CJ examined many of the other authorities since *Warren*. In his judgment he endorsed the pro-forma used by Northumbria police and said that there was a danger of putting *a new and heretical gloss* on the statute itself. His lordship held that there were many things which drivers ought to be told, but they need not be told them all at once. In addition there was no requirement for an officer to explain to a defendant *at the time of making a decision under s. 7(4)* that any blood sample taken would only be so taken by a doctor.

In *DPP v Jackson; Stanley v DPP* [1999] 1 AC 406, the House of Lords stressed the distinction between the roles of the police officer and the doctor. The police officer decides *which* evidential sample(s) should be

---

obtained and the medical practitioner decides *on the validity of the reasons put forward by the defendant* as to why a specimen of blood should not be taken. With three exceptions, the rules laid down in *Warren* were not mandatory elements of the procedure for taking evidential specimens but were guidelines indicating matters which should be brought to a defendant's attention before he/she exercised any choice that might be available.

The two elements that are mandatory are:

- in a s. 7(3) case (**see para. 3.5.5.1**), the warning required under s. 7(7) (**see para. 3.5.5.5**); and
- a statement as to why, in a case under s. 7(3), a breath specimen could not be used.

It would seem from the Divisional Court's decision in *Bobin* v *DPP* [1999] RTR 375 that, as long as the information set out above is provided by a police officer, it does not matter *which* police officer. Therefore, the warning under s. 7(7) might be given by, for instance, the arresting officer or by the custody officer who makes the requirement for the relevant specimen.

3.5.5.7 What Information Should Be Given to a Defendant?

As with other decisions involving when and where to give information to a defendant, there are probably fewer dangers in giving more than is required, sooner than required, than vice versa. Many of the cases before and since *Warren* have turned on the fact that drivers claim that they were not given the chance to reveal medical reasons as to why they could not give blood, or that they were not told that it would be a doctor who took the blood rather than a police officer. Such opportunity and information need not be given out as a general requirement although there seems to be little harm in following an approach that errs on the side of caution.

The officer should explain what the options are and that the decision as to which will be chosen is the officer's; the driver should also be given the opportunity to state any reasons why blood should not be taken so that the officer may take the appropriate advice (*Edge* v *DPP* [1993] RTR 146).

3.5.5.8 Requesting Medical Practitioners to Take a Specimen

The Road Traffic Act 1988, s. 7A states:

(1) A constable may make a request to a medical or health care practitioner for him to take a specimen of blood from a person ('the person concerned') irrespective of whether that person consents if—

    (a) that person is a person from whom the constable would (in the absence of any incapacity of that person and of any objection under section 9) be entitled under section 7 to require the provision of a specimen of blood for a laboratory test;

    (b) it appears to that constable that that person has been involved in an accident that constitutes or is comprised in the matter that is under investigation or the circumstances of that matter;

    (c) it appears to that constable that that person is or may be incapable (whether or not he has purported to do so) of giving a valid consent to the taking of a specimen of blood; and

    (d) it appears to that constable that that person's incapacity is attributable to medical reasons.

(2) A request under this section—

    (a) shall not be made to a medical or health care practitioner who for the time being has any responsibility (apart from the request) for the clinical care of the person concerned; and

    (b) shall not be made to a practitioner other than a police medical or health care practitioner unless—

        (i) it is not reasonably practicable for the request to be made to a police medical or health care practitioner; or

        (ii) it is not reasonably practicable for such a practitioner (assuming him to be willing to do so) to take the specimen.

(3) It shall be lawful for a medical or health care practitioner to whom a request is made under this section, if he thinks fit—

    (a) to take a specimen of blood from the person concerned irrespective of whether that person consents; and

    (b) to provide the sample to a constable.

This legislation came about as a result of the procedural difficulties encountered where suspected drivers are injured in an accident and, as a result, are incapable of giving their consent to the taking of a blood sample.

In order to prevent such drivers escaping conviction where they would otherwise have had to provide a blood sample, the legislation allows for the sample to be taken lawfully without consent at the time. Thereafter, the system relies on the driver giving his/her permission for the sample to be tested in a laboratory. It must appear to the constable that the person has been 'involved' in an accident, which is a far wider term than suspecting that the person was driving, attempting to drive or in charge of a vehicle at the time. However, the *reason* for the test will be important in determining the penalty available in the event that the person fails to give his/her consent (see para. 3.5.5.9).

It must also appear to the officer that the person is or may be *incapable* (as opposed to simply unwilling) of giving valid consent and that this incapacity is attributable to medical reasons (rather than other issues such as language or ethical objections).

As a general rule the doctor approached should be a police medical or health care practitioner. If it is not reasonably practicable either to make the request to the police medical or health care practitioner, or for the police medical or health care practitioner to take the sample, another medical or health care practitioner can be approached but not the medical or health care practitioner who has responsibility for the person's clinical care. The medical or health care practitioner is then empowered both to take the sample and to provide it to the officer without the person's consent if the medical or health care practitioner thinks fit, however, there is no obligation to do so.

A 'medical or health care practitioner' means a medical practitioner or a registered health care professional and 'police medical or health care practitioner' means a medical practitioner, or a registered health care professional, who is engaged under any agreement to provide medical or health care services for purposes connected with the activities of a police force.

The Road Traffic Act 1988, s. 7A goes on to state:

(4) If a specimen is taken in pursuance of a request under this section, the specimen shall not be subjected to a laboratory test unless the person from whom it was taken—
   (a) has been informed that it was taken; and
   (b) has been required by a constable to give his permission for a laboratory test of the specimen; and
   (c) has given his permission.

(5) A constable must, on requiring a person to give his permission for the purposes of this section for a laboratory test of a specimen, warn that person that a failure to give the permission may render him liable to prosecution.

The above requirements are critical if the analysis of any sample lawfully taken is to be of any evidential value. By implication, the requirement that the person give his/her permission to the sample being sent to a laboratory means that he/she should only be informed of the above matters and given the statutory warning once capable of understanding what is going on.

3.5.5.9 Failing to Give Permission for Test or Provide Specimen

OFFENCE: **Failing to Give Permission for Laboratory Test of Specimen—*Road Traffic Act 1988, s. 7A(6)***

• Triable summarily • If the test was for ascertaining ability to drive or the proportion of alcohol at the time the offender was driving or attempting to drive—six months' imprisonment and/or a fine and obligatory disqualification • In any other case, three months' imprisonment and/or a fine and discretionary disqualification

The Road Traffic Act 1988, s. 7A states:

(6) A person who, without reasonable excuse, fails to give his permission for a laboratory test of a specimen of blood taken from him under this section is guilty of an offence.

KEYNOTE

For a discussion of what may amount to reasonable excuse, see para. 3.5.5.11. However, there should be far fewer opportunities for claiming reasonable excuses here given that there is no technical equipment involved. The permission being given (or not) is for the laboratory analysis, *not* the taking of the specimen. Therefore delaying the giving of permission in order to obtain legal advice may be acceptable, particularly as, once the specimen has been taken and properly stored, there is not the same urgency as there is with the *taking* of a specimen before the alcohol/drugs dissipate. 'Failing' includes refusing (s. 11(2)).

3.5.5.10 Breath Specimen Showing Higher Alcohol Level to be Disregarded

The Road Traffic Act 1988, s. 8 states:

(1) Of any two specimens of breath provided by any person in pursuance of section 7 of this Act that with the lower proportion of alcohol in the breath shall be used and the other shall be disregarded.

KEYNOTE

It is standard practice that a driver provides two evidential breath samples. For charging and court purposes the higher reading will be disregarded and the lower used.

3.5.5.11 Failing to Provide an Evidential Specimen

OFFENCE: **Failing to Provide Evidential Specimen—*Road Traffic Act 1988, s. 7(6)***
 • Triable summarily • Six months' imprisonment and/or a fine • Obligatory disqualification

The Road Traffic Act 1988, s. 7 states:

(6) A person who, without reasonable excuse, fails to provide a specimen when required to do so in pursuance of this section is guilty of an offence.

KEYNOTE

Section 11(3) of the Road Traffic Act 1988 states that a breath specimen must be provided in such a way as to enable the analysis to be carried out. If a driver produces it in any other way, he/she will have 'failed to provide'. Provision of only one specimen of breath is a 'failure to provide' (*Cracknell* v *Willis* [1988] AC 450).

As with preliminary breath tests, 'fail' will include a refusal.

A person's general conduct in answer to a lawful requirement to provide a specimen, or a conditional response (e.g. 'I'm only providing a specimen if...) can amount to a refusal. The Court of Appeal has held that any such conduct or any such 'condition' does not need to be outrageous (cf. *R* v *Mackey* [1977] RTR 146). The key issue when considering any condition imposed by a driver before compliance is whether it amounted to a reasonable excuse for failure to comply with the test.

Reasonable Excuse

What amounts to a 'reasonable excuse' is a matter of law (see *Falzarano* below); whether the defendant actually *had* such an excuse is a question of fact for the court to determine having regard to the particular circumstances in each case.

In *DPP* v *Furby* [2000] RTR 181, it was held that if a police officer required a motorist to provide a breath specimen at the police station and the motorist made no effort at all to blow into the machine, he/she could not subsequently argue that he/she had a reasonable excuse for failing to do so. This principle was re-stated by the Administrative Court in a case where the driver alleged at the roadside that he suffered from bronchitis and therefore could not provide a breath sample. The arresting officer did not tell the custody officer of this alleged condition, neither did the motorist himself. As a result, the court held that no objective observer could say that the custody officer had 'reasonable cause to believe that for medical reasons a specimen of breath should not be required' and therefore the defendant should have been convicted for failing to provide a specimen (*DPP* v *Lonsdale* [2001] EWHC 95 (Admin)).

Although the choice under s. 7(4) is to be made by the requesting officer, the possibility of medical reasons for not giving blood must still be considered. An alleged fear of needles by the driver is a relevant consideration when making a decision as to whether a blood sample should be taken (*DPP* v *Jackson*; *Stanley* v *DPP* [1999] 1 AC 406 at **para. 3.5.5.6, Keynote** and also *Johnson* v *West Yorkshire Metropolitan Police* [1986] RTR 167). The driver should be given the opportunity to state any medical reasons why blood should not be taken but failure to give the driver that opportunity will not necessarily be fatal to an ensuing prosecution (*DPP* v *Orchard* [2000] All ER (D) 1457). However, any such reasons should be raised promptly. Where a driver clearly declined the option of replacing the breath specimen with a blood or urine sample, he was not permitted to claim later that a phobia of needles had caused him to decline the opportunity (*R (On the Application of Ijaz)* v *DPP* [2004] EWHC 2635 (Admin)).

The issues arising where a defendant claims to have had a 'reasonable excuse' for failing to provide a specimen of breath were reviewed by the Divisional Court in *DPP* v *Falzarano* [2001] RTR 14.

In *Falzarano* magistrates had accepted the defendant's claim that she was physically unable to provide the specimen as she was suffering from a panic attack. The defendant proved that she had a history of such attacks and that she was receiving medical treatment for the condition. Despite evidence from her own doctor that the condition and her failure to take her medication on the day in question should not have prevented her from providing a specimen of breath, the magistrates found that she did in fact have a reasonable excuse. On appeal by way of case stated, the Divisional Court held that:

- The 'reasonable excuse' had to arise out of a physical or mental inability to provide a specimen or a substantial risk to health in its provision (*R* v *Lennard* [1973] RTR 252).
- The evidence in support of the 'reasonable excuse' normally had to be medical but the defendant could provide it him/herself.
- There had to be a causative link between the excuse and the failure to provide a specimen (*DPP* v *Pearman* [1992] RTR 407).
- Being drunk or under stress was not in itself enough to provide a 'reasonable excuse' for failing to provide a specimen.
- Having considered the medical evidence, legal advice from their clerk and the demeanour of the defendant when testifying, the magistrates had been entitled on the evidence to find that *Falzarano* had a reasonable excuse for failing to provide breath specimens.

This decision does *not* mean that shortness of breath caused by panic attacks or stress will always amount to a reasonable excuse.

In assessing a highly unusual and creative defence to s. 7(6), the Divisional Court was not prepared to accept that seeing blood would have sent the defendant, a registered member of the Zimbabwe National Traditional Healers Association, into a trance whereby he could be violent to himself and others. A refusal to provide a blood specimen for such 'spiritual reasons' was not a reasonable excuse on the facts of this case (*DPP* v *Mukandiwa* [2005] EWHC 2977 (Admin)).

There have been many cases where 'excuses' have been put forward. The following is a brief summary:

Not Reasonable

- Refusal until legal advice has been sought; *Campbell* v *DPP* [2002] EWHC 1314 (Admin). This was reiterated by the Divisional Court in *Kennedy* v *DPP* [2002] EWHC 2297 (Admin) where it was held that the public interest required that the obtaining of specimens should not be delayed in this way. It would seem that this would include where a solicitor was ready and immediately available (*Chalupa* v *CPS* [2009] EWHC 3082 (Admin)).
- The absence of an appropriate adult where the defendant is a juvenile (*DPP* v *Evans* [2002] EWHC 2976 (Admin)).
- Refusal until solicitor present.
- Refusal on advice by solicitor.
- Refusal until driver had read the Codes of Practice under PACE.
- Mistaken belief by the defendant.
- Belief that the officer did not have the authority to make the requirement.
- Religious beliefs.
- Self-induced intoxication.
- Mental anguish caused by custody officer's behaviour.

Reasonable

- Mental incapacity.
- Physical incapacity.
- Inability to understand requirement caused by factors other than drink or drugs (e.g. language barrier).

Where any physical or mental incapacity (to provide the specimen or to understand the warning which accompanies it) is put forward, there will need to be clear, independent support for the claim being genuine (e.g. from a medical practitioner). Where a defendant's mental capacity to understand the warning is impaired by drunkenness, this is not a 'reasonable' excuse (*DPP* v *Beech* [1992] RTR 239).

The courts have warned of the need for caution when accepting a defendant's claim of such incapacity, particularly given the generally stressful nature of the police station procedure, together with the possible effects following an accident or motoring incident leading up to the request.

3.5.6 Hospital Procedure

The Road Traffic Act 1988, s. 9 states:

(1) While a person is at a hospital as a patient he shall not be required to co-operate with a preliminary test or to provide a specimen under section 7 of this Act unless the medical practitioner in immediate charge of his case has been notified of the proposal to make the requirement; and—
   (a) if the requirement is then made, it shall be for the provision of a specimen at the hospital, but
   (b) if the medical practitioner objects on the ground specified in subsection (2) below, the requirement shall not be made.

(1A) While a person is at a hospital as a patient, no specimen of blood shall be taken from him under section 7A of this Act and he shall not be required to give his permission for a laboratory test of a specimen taken under that section unless the medical practitioner in immediate charge of his case—
   (a) has been notified of the proposal to take the specimen or to make the requirement; and
   (b) has not objected on the ground specified in subsection (2).

(2) The ground on which the medical practitioner may object is—
   (a) in a case falling within subsection (1), that the requirement or the provision of the specimen or (if one is required) the warning required by section 7(7) of this Act would be prejudicial to the proper care and treatment of the patient; and
   (b) in a case falling within subsection (1A), that the taking of the specimen, the requirement or the warning required by section 7A(5) of this Act would be so prejudicial.

Note that a requirement to provide evidential *breath* specimens can be made at a hospital (**see para. 3.5.5.2**).

A 'hospital' is an institution which provides medical and surgical treatment for in-patients or out-patients (s. 11(2) of the Road Traffic Act 1988). It will also include anywhere within the precincts of that hospital, e.g. the hospital car park (*Attorney-General's Reference (No. 1 of 1976)* [1977] RTR 284).

Whether the person is there as a 'patient' or in another capacity will be a question of fact. In assessing this fact the courts will be helped by reference to hospital records which show names of patients, together with their times of admission and discharge (*Askew* v *DPP* [1988] RTR 303), although these records will not be conclusive.

If a person has been treated and then discharged from the hospital, he/she ceases to be a 'patient' for these purposes even if he/she has to return at a future date for further, related treatment (e.g. to have stitches removed).

Section 9(1A) was inserted in order to deal with the situations where a doctor has taken a blood specimen from the patient without his/her consent (under s. 7A, **see para. 3.5.5.8**). The overall effect of s. 7A and the above provision is that both the doctor taking the sample and the doctor in immediate charge of the patient need to be two separate people, both of whom will have to agree to the taking of the specimen. The 'medical practitioner in immediate charge of his case' was examined in *Cherpion* v *DPP* [2013] EWHC 615 (Admin) where the defence sought to claim that the doctor who gave permission for the specimen to be taken could not have been in immediate charge as she was a specialist. Although the doctor was not an A&E doctor she was the doctor the officer first saw at the hospital. The High Court held that the magistrates were right to take a common-sense view that this doctor was in immediate charge even though she was an orthopaedic surgeon.

In *Webber* v *DPP* [1998] RTR 111, the driver of a vehicle involved in an accident was taken to a hospital and registered as a patient. At the hospital she was requested to provide a preliminary breath test under s. 6. She refused and was therefore required to provide a blood sample but before she was able to provide the specimen, she was discharged. She was then arrested under s. 6 as a result of her earlier refusal. The driver was taken to a police station where she provided a specimen of blood on the strength of which she was subsequently convicted of driving while over the prescribed limit. She appealed, by way of case stated, on the ground that s. 9(1)(a) required the blood specimen to be taken at the *hospital*, which in this case it was not. The Divisional Court held that, once the obligation to provide a specimen for analysis has been made, it is not to be discharged simply by an 'irrelevant change of *locus*'. The court went on to say that by making the requirement, the police officer set in train a procedure which carries a sanction (s. 7(6)), a procedure that was not to be altered by the mere fact that the defendant, for whatever reason, had left the hospital before complying with the requirement.

The restriction applies to both preliminary breath tests and evidential tests.

If the patient provides a positive reading or fails to provide a specimen of breath, he/she cannot then be arrested while still a 'patient' (s. 6D(3)).

3.5.7 Detention of Person Affected

The Road Traffic Act 1988, s. 10 states:

(1) Subject to subsections (2) and (3) below, a person required under section 7 or 7A to provide a specimen of breath, blood or urine may afterwards be detained at a police station (or, if the specimen was provided otherwise than at a police station, arrested and taken to and detained at a police station) if a constable has reasonable grounds for believing that, were that person then driving or attempting to drive a mechanically propelled vehicle on a road, he would commit an offence under section 4, 5 or 5A of this Act.

(2) Subsection (1) above does not apply to the person if it ought reasonably to appear to the constable that there is no likelihood of his driving or attempting to drive a mechanically propelled vehicle whilst—

(a) the person's ability to drive properly is impaired,

(b) the proportion of alcohol in the person's breath, blood or urine exceeds the prescribed limit, or

(c) the proportion of a specified controlled drug in the person's blood or urine exceeds the specified limit for that drug.

(2A) A person who is at a hospital as a patient shall not be arrested and taken from there to a police station in pursuance of this section if it would be prejudicial to his proper care and treatment as a patient.

(3) A constable must consult a medical practitioner on any question arising under this section whether a person's ability to drive properly is or might be impaired through drugs and must act on the medical practitioner's advice.

KEYNOTE

The wording of this section means that this is a *subjective* test and the officer must be able to point to the 'reasonable grounds' for his/her belief. It is possible that a further screening test might provide such grounds but there is no specific requirement or power for this test to take place.

If it ought reasonably to appear to the officer (another *subjective* test) that there is no likelihood of the person driving/attempting to drive such a vehicle while impaired or over the prescribed limit, the power to arrest and/or detain under s. 10(1) does *not apply* and the person cannot be further detained under this section.

While effective, the practice of retaining the person's car keys after their release is not authorised by s. 10.

3.6 | Insurance

3.6.1 Introduction

Every person using, or causing or permitting another person to use a motor vehicle on a road or other public place, necessarily presents an element of risk to others. With regard to that risk there is a requirement that most road users are insured against third party risk.

3.6.2 Requirement for Insurance or Security

The Road Traffic Act 1988, s. 143 states:

> (1) Subject to the provisions of this Part of this Act—
>   (a) a person must not use a motor vehicle on a road or other public place unless there is in force in relation to the use of the vehicle by that person such a policy of insurance or such a security in respect of third party risks as complies with the requirements of this Part of this Act, and
>   (b) a person must not cause or permit any other person to use a motor vehicle on a road or other public place unless there is in force in relation to the use of the vehicle by that other person such a policy of insurance or such a security in respect of third party risks as complies with the requirements of this Part of this Act.

OFFENCE: **Contravening Requirement for Insurance—*Road Traffic Act 1988, s. 143(2)***
* Triable summarily * Fine * Discretionary disqualification

The Road Traffic Act 1988, s. 143 states:

> (2) If a person acts in contravention of subsection (1) above he is guilty of an offence.

KEYNOTE

The policy behind s. 143 is to safeguard road users and pedestrians from uninsured injury from motor vehicles, by providing for compulsory insurance (*Winter* v *DPP* [2002] EWHC 1524 (Admin)). In deciding whether a particular conveyance or contraption is a 'motor vehicle' and needs insurance or not, the court will have this feature firmly in mind. Unless the insurer of a vehicle delivers a certificate of insurance to the person taking out the policy, the requirements of s. 143(1) will not have been met (s. 147(1)). Therefore, anyone using, or causing or permitting to be used, a motor vehicle on a road or other public place before the delivery of such a certificate, commits this offence. Delivery may take place electronically so that a certificate of insurance transmitted from the insurer to the insured by email or made available for access on a website is sufficient (s. 147(1A)(a) and (b)).

Many insurance companies issue instant insurance cover over the telephone by creating an 'agency' to which the insurance certificate is delivered on behalf of the insured. As the agency effectively receives the certificate on the insured's behalf, this gets around the requirement of having to deliver the certificate before the insurance becomes effective as referred to above.

A driver may be required under s. 165 or s. 170 of the Road Traffic Act 1988 to produce a certificate of insurance (or other acceptable form of security) (see chapter 3.2). In such cases, in order to determine whether a motor vehicle was being driven in contravention of s. 143, s. 171 of the Road Traffic Act 1988 places a requirement on the *owner* of the vehicle to give such information as required by the police. Failure to comply with such a requirement is a summary offence. However, where a defendant is charged with driving without insurance, once the prosecution have proved that the defendant has driven on a public highway, it is for the defendant to show that he/she had insurance and there is no obligation on the police to serve any request for production of the relevant documentation (e.g. an HORT/1)—*DPP* v *Hay* [2005] EWHC 1395 (Admin).

The risks which must be covered by any insurance policy for the purposes of s. 143 are set out in s. 145(3). These are generally:

* Liability in relation to bodily injury caused to others when the vehicle is on a road in Great Britain.
* Civil liability in relation to the use of a vehicle from another EU Member State in Great Britain.
* Civil liability in relation to the use of a vehicle from Great Britain in another EU Member State.

If a claim is made against a motorist in respect of any such liability required to be covered by a policy of insurance, the motorist has a number of legal obligations. In essence, the motorist must, on demand by or on behalf of the person making the claim:

(a) state whether or not:
    (i) he/she was insured (or had in force a security) having effect for the purpose of the Act or
    (ii) he/she would have been insured (or had in force such a security) if the insurer (or the giver of the security) had not avoided or cancelled the policy or security, and

(b) if he/she was (or would have been) so insured, or had or would have had in force such a security, he/she must:
    (i) give relevant particulars with respect to that policy or security as specified in any certificate of insurance or security delivered in respect of that policy or security under s. 147;
    (ii) where no such certificate was delivered under s. 147, give particulars of the registration mark, the number of the insurance policy, the name of the insurer and the period of the insurance cover.

It would appear that this risk extends to the owner of a hamburger van who walked into the path of an oncoming motorcyclist after stepping into the road when displaying a sign for the business. The incident was closely linked to 'using the van on the road' as a hamburger van (*Christopher Wastell* v *The Estate of Gordon John Woodward, Deceased (1) and Chaucer Syndicates Ltd* (2017) unreported).

A local authority has the power (under s. 222 of the Local Government Act 1972) to bring a criminal prosecution for the offence of driving without insurance contrary to s. 143 of the Road Traffic Act 1988 (*Middlesbrough Borough Council* v *Safeer* [2001] EWHC Admin 525).

3.6.2.1 Strict Liability

Generally the offence under s. 143 is one of strict liability, that is, you need not prove any intent or guilty knowledge by the defendant in order to convict (*Tapsell* v *Maslen* [1967] Crim LR 53).

If, however, a person allows another to use his/her vehicle on the express condition that the other person insures it first, the lender cannot be convicted of 'permitting' (*Newbury* v *Davis* [1974] RTR 367).

KEYNOTE

However, there is still a burden of proof on the Crown to prove that the use of the vehicle had not been in accordance with the terms of use permitted by that policy of insurance. In *DPP* v *Whittaker* [2015] EWHC 1850 (Admin) the defendant was stopped by police while driving a van containing a large number of DVDs. There was limited questioning by the police officer about the use of the vehicle and the defendant subsequently produced a valid certificate of motor insurance permitting social domestic and pleasure use of the van. The defendant was charged with using a motor vehicle without insurance on the basis that the van was used for the business of mobile DVD sales which was not permitted under the terms of insurance. The Justices found no case to answer which was supported by the High Court, holding that the prosecution still had to provide evidence that the vehicle was being used for a business use to discharge their burden of proof.

3.6.2.2 Defence

The Road Traffic Act 1988, s. 143 states:

(3) A person charged with using a motor vehicle in contravention of this section shall not be convicted if he proves—

    (a) that the vehicle did not belong to him and was not in his possession under a contract of hiring or of loan,

    (b) that he was using the vehicle in the course of his employment, and

    (c) that he neither knew nor had reason to believe that there was not in force in relation to the vehicle such a policy of insurance or security as is mentioned in subsection (1) above.

KEYNOTE

Note that if the driver is employed by the vehicle's owner you must prove that the driver was acting in the course of his/her employment before you can convict the owner of using, causing or permitting the use of the vehicle without insurance. The driver's own inadmissible statement to that effect will not suffice (*Jones* v *DPP* [1999] RTR 1).

The burden of proof in such a case is on the defendant and will be judged on the balance of probabilities (*R* v *Carr-Briant* [1943] KB 607).

3.6.2.3 Insurance Policy

The form in which certificates must appear, together with the requirement for insurers to keep and supply copies of records, are contained in the Motor Vehicles (Third Party Risks) Regulations 1972 (SI 1972/1217) as amended.

Cover notes are included, by s. 161(1) of the Road Traffic Act 1988, in the meaning of 'policy of insurance'.

The internationally recognised 'green card scheme' allows for the insurance of British vehicles abroad and overseas vehicles in Great Britain (see the Motor Vehicles (International Motor Insurance Card) Regulations 1971 (SI 1971/792)).

The requirement (under s. 145(3)(b) of the 1988 Act) removes the need for the 'green card' scheme within the EU for vehicles from Member States.

If a policy is restricted to a named person, only that person will generally be covered by it.

If, as often happens, the policy covers any person who holds a current driving licence, that description may include the holder of a provisional licence (*Rendlesham* v *Dunne* [1964] 1 Lloyd's Rep 192) or even the holder of a licence issued in another country.

If a policy refers to 'agents' or 'employees', you will need to establish whether or not the relevant person fits into those categories. Garage proprietors returning vehicles to the owner after repairing them are not in the owner's employment (*Lyons* v *May* [1948] 2 All ER 1062). However, an employee driving an employer's vehicle in an unauthorised manner will not negate the effect of a policy of insurance (*Marsh* v *Moores* [1949] 2 KB 208).

Generally, an insurance policy obtained by false representations will be valid for the purposes of s. 143 and will remain so until the contract has been 'avoided' (ended) by the insurer (*Durrant* v *MacLaren* [1956] 2 Lloyd's Rep 70).

Although the question of whether or not a policy applies to the particular vehicle will not usually present a problem, trailers can create difficulties, in relation to both the vehicles covered by the policy, and the use to which they are being put. Trailers are themselves 'vehicles' and may be included in the definition of motor vehicle when charging an offence under s. 143 (*Rogerson* v *Stephens* [1950] 2 All ER 144).

Insurance policies will often exclude certain uses (e.g. racing and time trials). The particular wording of each policy is important when determining any purpose that is expressly included or excluded and many policies use the wording 'social and domestic purposes'. Lending vehicles to friends in return for payment reimbursing petrol costs will amount to a social and domestic purpose, as will using the vehicle to help a friend move house (*Lee* v *Poole* [1954] Crim LR 942).

'Social and domestic' does not include business trips (*Wood* v *General Accident etc. Assurance Co.* (1948) 65 TLR 53).

Insurance cover in respect of 'the insured's business' does not extend to other businesses of friends or colleagues (*Passmore* v *Vulcan etc. Insurance Co.* (1935) 154 LT 258).

If employees deviate from the ordinary course of their duties or employment, on what is often termed a 'frolic of their own', they may not be covered by the terms of the employer's policy. Simply taking a two-mile detour in order to give someone a lift has been held not to invalidate the employer's insurance policy (*Ballance* v *Brown* [1955] Crim LR 384) but each case will have to be decided on its own facts.

Although many policies exclude use of the particular vehicle for payment or reward, s. 150 of the 1988 Act makes provision for 'car-sharing' agreements, provided that they meet the criteria set out.

Clearly any insurance policy must be shown to have been in force at the relevant time. Many business users have arrangements whereby they pass the risk to their insurers at short notice and it will always be necessary to establish whether a particular policy is actually operative at the time (see e.g. *Samuelson* v *National Insurance etc. Ltd* [1986] 3 All ER 417).

3.6.2.4 Exclusions

Section 148(1) of the Road Traffic Act 1988 makes the effects of some restrictions in a policy void in relation to s. 143. This means that, if a policy purports to restrict the extent of its cover by reference to any of these features, breach of them by the insured person will not affect the validity of that policy for the purposes of s. 143.

Those features (under s. 148) are:

(2) ...
    (a) the age or physical or mental condition of persons driving the vehicle,
    (b) the condition of the vehicle,
    (c) the number of persons that the vehicle carries,
    (d) the weight or physical characteristics of the goods that the vehicle carries,
    (e) the time at which or the areas within which the vehicle is used,
    (f) the horsepower or cylinder capacity or value of the vehicle,
    (g) the carrying on the vehicle of any particular apparatus, or
    (h) the carrying on the vehicle of any particular means of identification other than any means of identification required to be carried by or under the Vehicle Excise and Registration Act 1994.

3.6.2.5 Exemptions

Crown vehicles do not appear to require insurance *while being used as such*; if they are being used for some other purpose, they will need insurance on a road or public place.

Section 144 of the 1988 Act sets out other occasions where vehicles will be exempt. Such occasions include police authority vehicles and vehicles being used for police purposes; this will include off duty police officers using their own vehicle for police purposes (*Jones* v *Chief Constable of Bedfordshire* [1987] RTR 332).

3.6.2.6 Disclosure of Information about Insurance Status of Vehicles

Under s. 153 of the Serious Organised Crime and Police Act 2005 the Secretary of State made provision for requiring the Motor Insurers' Information Centre (MIIC—a company limited by guarantee) to make available 'relevant vehicle insurance information' to the police with a view to making that information available for use by constables. 'Relevant vehicle insurance information' means information (in any form) relating to vehicles that have previously been, but are no longer, insured under a policy of insurance (or security in respect of third party risks) complying with the relevant requirements of the Road Traffic Act 1988. This information will be set out in a 'periodic data list' taken from the motor insurance database. Effectively the legislation enables the police to have access to insurance industry data relating to vehicles whose use is no longer insured. The police are also able to link the processed data to Automated Number-Plate Reader (ANPR) units to assist them in detecting people driving without insurance.

Regulation 3 requires the MIIC to provide a list of vehicles, the use of which was covered by a policy of insurance on the reference date (a date before the periodic data list was produced) but is no longer covered under such a policy when the list is generated. The information which must be provided is the:

- registration mark
- make and model (where available to the MIIC) and
- date on which the vehicle ceased to have a record of insurance on the database.

Police officers may use the processed information to assist them in deciding whether to use their powers under s. 165 of the 1988 Act to require a person who is, or may have been, driving a vehicle to produce evidence that the vehicle is insured.

Any information provided to police officers should not be further disclosed by them except for the purposes of legal proceedings for contravening the 1988 Act or legislation made under it.

3.6.3 Motor Insurers' Bureau

All insurers in Great Britain are required to be members of the Motor Insurers' Bureau (MIB) (s. 145 of the Road Traffic Act 1988).

The purpose of the MIB is to provide compensation where someone is unable to pursue a valid claim against another following a road traffic accident because the other party is:

- not insured
- not known/traceable
- insured by a company now in liquidation.

The MIB has drawn up an agreement with the Secretary of State which sets out its terms of operation. Generally it will not pay compensation to those who are victims of deliberate criminal acts involving motor vehicles (including those who allow themselves to be carried in vehicles taken without the owner's consent), neither will it compensate those who 'use' vehicles without insurance ('use' here will be taken in the wide sense discussed in **chapter 3.1** and will include some passengers (see e.g. *Stinton* v *Stinton* [1995] RTR 167 and *O'Mahoney* v *Joliffe and Motor Insurers' Bureau* [1999] RTR 245)). The Court of Appeal decided that a person injured by an uninsured or untraced driver cannot enforce a claim for compensation against the MIB by citing the 'direct effect' of EC Council Directive 84/5 which provides certain rights for citizens of EU Member States (*Mighell* v *Reading*; *Evans* v *Motor Insurers' Bureau*; *White* v *White* [1999] Lloyd's Rep IR 30).

The MIB scheme generates a considerable amount of civil litigation that, on the whole, is of little direct importance to police officers. However, there are key evidential areas that may arise during the course of an investigation into accidents and collisions. For instance, the MIB will generally deny liability for any damages or loss to passengers who knew, or ought to have known, that the driver was uninsured. Evidence of conversations between passengers and drivers before and during any journeys can therefore become highly relevant in subsequent litigation (see e.g. *Akers* v *Motor Insurers' Bureau* [2003] EWCA Civ 18).

In order to help people seeking compensation generally for motor accidents across the European Economic Area, Member States have set up clearing houses where insurance information relating to vehicles within the relevant country is pooled. In the United Kingdom, the Motor Insurers' Information Centre (MIIC) has been set up for this purpose. Following an accident, a person in the relevant Member State will be entitled to specific information regarding the vehicle(s) and insurance policy details on application. Full details of the scheme, along with the entitlement to compensation and the role of the MIB within the scheme can be found in the Motor Vehicles (Compulsory Insurance) (Information Centre and Compensation Body) Regulations 2003 (SI 2003/37).

3.7 | Legislation for the Protection of Road Users

3.7.1 Introduction

Safety considerations are uppermost in road policing and this chapter deals with the main areas of legislation aimed at increasing and enforcing safety for all road users whether they are in or on a vehicle or using the roads or highways for any legitimate purpose.

3.7.2 Seat Belts

Seat belt legislation is age and height specific, the current arrangements are summarised below:

	Seat belt usage in front seat	Seat belt usage in rear seat	Responsible for compliance
Driver	Must be worn if fitted	N/A	Driver
Children under 3 years old	Must use an appropriate child restraint	Must use an appropriate child restraint. Must use adult belt if: – In a taxi, the correct child restraint not available – On a short and occasional trip, the correct child restraint not available – Two occupied child restraints prevent fitment of a third	Driver
Children aged 3 and above, until they reach EITHER their 12th birthday OR 135 cm in height	Must use an appropriate child restraint	Must use an appropriate child restraint	Driver
Children over 135 cm in height, or who are 12 or 13 years old	Must be worn if fitted	Must be worn if fitted	Driver
Adult passengers aged 14 and over	Must be worn if fitted.	Must be worn if fitted	Passenger

Height-based seats, known as 'i-Size' seats, must be rear-facing until the child is over 15 months old. The child can use a forward-facing child car seat when they are over 15 months old.

Weight-based seats: the seat a child can use (and the way they must be restrained in it) depends on their weight.

Child's weight	Group	Seats
0 kg to 9 kg	0	Lie-flat or 'lateral' baby carrier, rear-facing baby carrier or rear-facing baby seat using a harness
0 kg to 13 kg	0+	Rear-facing baby carrier or rear-facing baby seat using a harness
9 kg to 18 kg	1	Rear- or forward-facing baby seat using a harness or safety shield
15 kg to 36 kg	2 and 3	Rear- or forward-facing child car seat (high-backed booster seat or booster cushion) using a seat belt, harness or safety shield

These new seats must also not be backless booster seats for children less than 125 cm tall or weighing under 22 kg. This applies to new seats manufactured post-March 2017 and not to existing seats.

3.7.2.1 Fitting of Seat Belts

The law governing the fitting of seat belts is currently set out in regs 46 to 47 of the Road Vehicles (Construction and Use) Regulations 1986 (SI 1986/1078), as amended.

All cars first registered after 1 January 1965 must be fitted with seat belts in the front seats. Cars manufactured after 1 October 1981 must have anchor points fitted for rear seat belts. Cars manufactured after 1 October 1986 and first registered after 1 April 1987 must be fitted with rear seat belts. The regulations also require a seat belt to be fitted in the centre front seat of cars and light vans where such a seat is provided.

The Regulations allow for different types of belt or restraint to be fitted in order to meet European obligations and to allow individuals to choose the most suitable type of belt for themselves or restraint for their children.

Regulation 48 outlines the requirements for the maintenance of seat belts and anchorage points.

3.7.2.2 Wearing of Seat Belts by Adults

OFFENCE: **Contravention of Regulation Relating to Seat Belts—*Road Traffic Act 1988, s. 14(3)***
- Triable summarily • Fine

The Road Traffic Act 1988, s. 14(3) states:

> A person who drives or rides in a motor vehicle in contravention of regulations under this section is guilty of an offence; but, notwithstanding any enactment or rule of law, no person other than the person actually committing the contravention is guilty of an offence by reason of the contravention.

In summary, the general rules for adults are:

- when travelling in the front seat of any vehicle, an adult must wear a seat belt if one is available; and
- when travelling in the back seat of a car an adult must wear a seat belt if it is available.

This legislation applies to person aged 14 years or over.

The legislation makes it clear that no person *other than the person actually committing the contravention* is guilty of an offence by reason of the contravention. This means that, irrespective of the general law relating to the aiding and abetting of offences, the driver of a vehicle will not be responsible for a passenger not wearing a seat belt.

3.7.2.3 Wearing of Restraints by Children

The law governing the wearing of seat belts by children travelling in the front of a car is currently set out in the Motor Vehicles (Wearing of Seat Belts by Children in Front Seats)

Regulations 1993 (SI 1993/31), as amended, while the wearing of restraints by children travelling in the rear of a car is currently set out in the Motor Vehicles (Wearing of Seat Belts) Regulations 1993 (SI 1993/176), as amended.

In summary, the general rules for children are:

- no child may be carried unrestrained in the front seat of any vehicle;
- all children under three years old must use an appropriate child restraint when travelling in a car;
- children under 12 and less than 135 cm must be seated in the rear of the vehicle in an appropriate restraint, if no restraint is available the child cannot travel in the car;
- children between the ages of 12 and 14 must wear an appropriate restraint in the rear of a vehicle if one is provided and must move to the front if there is no seat belt in the rear but there is one available in the front.

There are three offences in relation to carrying a child in a car without wearing a seat belt; they are all covered by s. 15 of the Road Traffic Act 1988.

OFFENCE: **Driving Motor Vehicle in Contravention of Requirement for Seat Belts for under 14s—*Road Traffic Act 1988, s. 15***
- Triable summarily • Fine

The Road Traffic Act 1988, s. 15 states:

(1) Except as provided by regulations, where a child under the age of fourteen years is in the front of a motor vehicle, a person must not without reasonable excuse drive the vehicle on a road unless the child is wearing a seat belt in conformity with regulations.

(1A) Where—
  (a) a child is in the front of a motor vehicle other than a bus,
  (b) the child is in a rear-facing child restraining device, and
  (c) the passenger seat where the child is placed is protected by a front air bag,
  a person must not without reasonable excuse drive the vehicle on a road unless the air bag is deactivated...

(3) Except as provided by regulations, where—
  (a) a child under the age of three years is in the rear of a motor vehicle, or
  (b) a child of or over that age but under the age of fourteen years is in the rear of a motor vehicle and any seat belt is fitted in the rear of that vehicle,
  a person must not without reasonable excuse drive the vehicle on a road unless the child is wearing a seat belt in conformity with regulations.

(3A) Except as provided by regulations, where—
  (a) a child who is under the age of 12 years and less than 150 centimetres in height is in the rear of a passenger car,
  (b) no seat belt is fitted in the rear of the passenger car, and
  (c) a seat in the front of the passenger car is provided with a seat belt but is not occupied by any person,
  a person must not without reasonable excuse drive the passenger car on a road.

KEYNOTE

The first offence relates to carrying a child in the front seat in a rear-facing child restraint in a vehicle fitted with an air bag. An air bag is regarded as 'deactivated' where it is designed or adapted in such a way that it cannot inflate enough to pose a risk of injury to a child travelling in a rear-facing child restraining device in the seat in question.

The second offence relates carrying a child under the age of 14 without the child wearing an appropriate child restraint.

The third relates to driving a 'passenger car' with a child in the back in a car with no rear seat belts fitted where the front seat is unoccupied. A passenger car is defined as:

a motor vehicle which—

(a) is constructed or adapted for use for the carriage of passengers and is not a goods vehicle,

(b) has no more than eight seats in addition to the driver's seat,

(c) has four or more wheels,

(d) has a maximum design speed exceeding 25 kilometres per hour, and

(e) has a maximum laden weight not exceeding 3.5 tonnes.

If a person drives in contravention of the regulations pertaining to children, he/she commits the offence under s. 15(2) or (4).

3.7.2.4 Exemptions

The following exemptions to wearing a seat belt apply by virtue of the Motor Vehicles (Wearing of Seat Belts) Regulations 1993:

- a person holding a medical certificate;
- the driver of or a passenger in a motor vehicle constructed or adapted for carrying goods, while on a journey which does not exceed 50 metres and which is undertaken for the purpose of delivering or collecting anything;
- a person riding in a motor ambulance whilst the person is providing medical attention or treatment to a patient which, due to its nature or the medical situation of the patient, cannot be delayed;
- a person driving a vehicle while performing a manoeuvre which includes reversing; a qualified driver (within the meaning given by reg. 17 of the Motor Vehicles (Driving Licences) Regulations 1999) who is supervising the holder of a provisional licence (within the meaning of part III of the Act) while that holder is performing a manoeuvre which includes reversing;
- a person by whom, as provided in the Motor Vehicles (Driving Licences) Regulations 1999, a test of competence to drive is being conducted and his wearing a seat belt would endanger himself or any other person;
- a person driving or riding in a vehicle while it is being used for fire brigade or, in England, fire and rescue authority or police purposes or for carrying a person in lawful custody (a person who is being so carried being included in this exemption);
- the driver of—
  (i) a licensed taxi while it is being used for seeking hire, or answering a call for hire, or carrying a passenger for hire, or
  (ii) a private hire vehicle while it is being used to carry a passenger for hire;
- a person riding in a vehicle, being used under a trade licence, for the purpose of investigating or remedying a mechanical fault in the vehicle;
- a disabled person who is wearing a disabled person's belt; or
- a person riding in a vehicle while it is taking part in a procession organised by or on behalf of the Crown.

In addition to these general exemptions, there are other occasions where the requirements will not apply. If there is no adult seat belt provided for the driver, or available for passengers aged 14 and over, the requirements will not apply (reg. 6).

Schedule 2 to the Regulations expands on a number of occasions where seat belts will be deemed not to be 'available'. These occasions include:

- where the seat is properly occupied by someone wearing the seat belt;
- where the seat is occupied by someone with a medical exemption.

If a person is unable to wear a seat belt owing to a disability, the seat belt will not be regarded for this purpose as being 'available'.

KEYNOTE

If a person holds a medical certificate signed by a doctor stating that the wearing of a seat belt by that person is inadvisable on medical grounds, that person will be exempt. Any such certificate must state the period over which it applies and carry the symbol prescribed in the regulations. If it is to be used in evidence in answer to a charge under s. 14(3) of the 1988 Act, such a certificate must be produced to a constable on request or to a police station within seven days (s. 14(4)).

3.7.3 Motor Cycle Helmets

Under s. 16 of the Road Traffic Act 1988, the Secretary of State may make Regulations relating to the wearing of protective headgear by people riding motor cycles of any class specified in the Regulations. A motor cycle is defined in s. 185(1) of the Road Traffic Act 1988 as 'a mechanically propelled vehicle, not being an invalid carriage, with less than four wheels and the weight of which unladen does not exceed 410 kilograms'.

The relevant regulations are the Motor Cycles (Protective Helmets) Regulations 1998 (SI 1998/1807) as amended. The Regulations require every person driving or riding on a motor *bicycle* on a road to wear protective headgear (reg. 4).

OFFENCE: **Driving or Riding on Motor Cycle in Contravention of Regulations— *Road Traffic Act 1988, s. 16(4)***
- Triable summarily • Fine

The Road Traffic Act 1988, s. 16 states:

(4) A person who drives or rides on a motor cycle in contravention of regulations under this section is guilty of an offence...

KEYNOTE

The Regulations do not apply to all motor cycles; they only apply to motor bicycles. A 'motor bicycle' is defined, for the purposes of the Regulations, by reg. 4, as 'a two-wheeled motor cycle, whether or not having a side-car attached' (any wheels the centres of which in contact with the road surface are less than 460mm apart are to be counted as one wheel).

Certain motor mowers are exempted by reg. 4(2) of the 1998 Regulations.

The helmet worn must either conform to one of the British Standards specified (in reg. 5) and be marked as such or it must give a similar (or greater) degree of protection as one which meets those Standards *and* be of a type manufactured for motor cyclists (reg. 4(3)(a)). If the helmet is unfastened or improperly fastened (e.g. with part of the chinstrap undone) the offence will be complete (reg. 4(3)(b) and (c)).

It is a summary offence under s. 17(2) to sell or let on hire a helmet for these purposes which does not meet the prescribed requirements. That offence will be committed even if the helmet is sold for off-road use (*Losexis Ltd* v *Clarke* [1984] RTR 174).

The wording of the Regulations suggests that no helmet is required by someone who is pushing a motor bicycle along but, if he/she straddled it and paddled it along with his/her feet, a helmet would be required (*Crank* v *Brooks* [1980] RTR 441).

Section 16(2) creates an exemption for 'a follower of the Sikh religion while he is wearing a turban'.

The Motor Cycles (Eye Protectors) Regulations 1999 (SI 1999/535) as amended create an offence (under s. 18(3)) of using non-prescribed eye protectors when driving or riding on a motor cycle. These Regulations do not require the use of eye protectors; they impose standards on those appliances which motor cyclists choose

3.7.3.1 Passengers

'Riding on' in the above offence means that pillion passengers must wear helmets but s. 16(1) of the 1988 Act exempts people in sidecars.

As with the seat belt provisions above, there is an exception to the general rule on aiding and abetting. Section 16(4) provides that only the person committing the offence of not wearing a helmet shall be liable *unless the person is under* 16. This means that, where a 16-year-old rider of a motor bicycle carries a 15-year-old pillion passenger who is not wearing a helmet, the 16-year-old will be responsible for the commission of the offence by the passenger as well as the passenger him/herself. If the passenger were 16 years old, he/she alone would be responsible for his/her offence.

OFFENCE: **Passengers on Motor Cycles—*Road Traffic Act 1988, s. 23***
- Triable summarily • Fine • Discretionary disqualification

The Road Traffic Act 1988, s. 23 states:

(1) Not more than one person in addition to the driver may be carried on a motor bicycle.
(2) No person in addition to the driver may be carried on a motor bicycle otherwise than sitting astride the motor cycle and on a proper seat securely fixed to the motor cycle behind the driver's seat.
(3) If a person is carried on a motor cycle in contravention of this section, the driver of the motor cycle is guilty of an offence.

KEYNOTE

Under this section it is the *driver* who commits the offence (s. 23(3)), and the passenger can be convicted of aiding and abetting.

There is no specific requirement for the passenger to face the *front*—though this is presumably because it did not occur to the legislators that anyone would be daft enough to face the other way. Any person travelling as a passenger astride a motor cycle but facing the rear may commit an offence under the Road Vehicles (Construction and Use) Regulations 1986; he/she may also commit an offence of aiding and abetting the driver to drive dangerously.

Note that under the 1986 Regulations suitable supports for a passenger must be provided on a motor bicycle if it is to carry a passenger (reg. 102). There is no requirement that the supports be used by a passenger.

3.7.4 Speeding and Speed Limits

Speed limits may apply to particular roads (e.g. 'restricted' roads), particular vehicles (e.g. heavy commercial vehicles) or temporary conditions imposed in a given area. There are also further conditions regulating speed limits on motorways. As a general rule, the limit on motorways and dual carriageways for most cars will be 70 mph. However, there are many exceptions, and local regulations and orders should be consulted in cases of doubt.

Generally, the approval of the Secretary of State is required before speed limits of any great duration are imposed. However, that requirement has been removed in relation to speed limits of 20 mph by the Road Traffic Regulation Act 1984 (Amendment) Order 1999 (SI 1999/1608). As a result of this and other legislation (including the Traffic Signs Regulations and General Directions 2002 (SI 2002/3113)), local traffic authorities can create 20 mph zones under certain circumstances within their jurisdiction as part of a traffic calming scheme. Full guidance on the creation of such zones can be found in DETR Circular 05/99.

Under the Transport Act 2000, local authorities are empowered to designate roads as 'quiet lanes' or 'home zones', thereby placing greater restrictions on the use of them.

Although the imposition of a specific speed limit is a matter for legislation (either primary or in regulations and orders), the enforcement of those limits is an operational matter for the police force involved. While there is therefore a great deal of room for discretion in the enforcement of speed limits and there will always be exceptional cases, NPCC has produced guidelines setting out the *minimum* speeds at which it suggests enforcement action should be taken.

The use of reflective or elaborately designed number plates to thwart speed cameras has been directly addressed in regulations.

The practice of drivers warning other motorists of the presence of a police speed detection operation can amount to an offence of obstructing a police constable in the execution of his/her duty. In such cases however it is critical that you can show that those warned were either exceeding the legal speed limit or were likely to do so at the location of the speed detection (*DPP* v *Glendinning* [2005] EWHC 2333 (Admin) and *Betts* v *Stevens* [1910] 1 KB 1). In the absence of any such evidence, merely giving a warning to fellow drivers who were observing the speed limit at the time will not amount to this offence (see also *Bastable* v *Little* [1907] 1 KB 59).

3.7.4.1 Speed Limits on Restricted Roads

Section 81(1) of the Road Traffic Regulation Act 1984 provides that the speed limit on a 'restricted road' will be 30 mph. A restricted road is then defined under s. 82 as follows:

(1) Subject to the provisions of this section and of section 84(3) of this Act, a road is a restricted road for the purposes of section 81 of this Act if—
    (a) in England and Wales, there is provided on it a system of street lighting furnished by means of lamps placed not more than 200 yards apart;
    (b) (applies to Scotland only).
(2) The traffic authority for a road may direct—
    (a) that the road which is a restricted road for the purposes of section 81 of this Act shall cease to be a restricted road for those purposes, or
    (b) that the road which is not a restricted road for those purposes shall become a restricted road for those purposes.

KEYNOTE

By virtue of s. 85(5), where a road has such a system of street lamps the lack of any traffic signs specifically saying that the road is not a 'restricted' road will be evidence that it *is* a 'restricted' road.

If there are no such street lamps then there must be traffic signs stating what the speed limit is (s. 85(4)).

Although the two subsections above clearly overlap, the traffic authority can use the power under s. 82(2)(b) to impose 'restricted' status (and therefore a speed limit of 30 mph) on a road even though the road does not have a system of lighting as set out in s. 82(1)(a) (*DPP* v *Evans* [2004] EWHC 2785 (Admin)).

3.7.4.2 Traffic Signs

The proper display of appropriate traffic signs is often critical to the enforcement of speed limits and successful prosecution for infringement.

The Road Traffic Regulation Act 1984, s. 85(1) states:

For the purpose of securing that adequate guidance is given to drivers of motor vehicles as to whether any, and if so what, limit of speed is to be observed on any road, it shall be the duty of the Secretary of State, [in the case of a road for which he is the traffic authority, to] erect and maintain…traffic signs in such positions as may be requisite for that purpose.

The Traffic Signs Regulations and General Directions 2016 set out the requirements for signs that are used, among other things, for speed limits, and the Traffic Signs Manual 2008 sets out how the signs approved by TSRGD are to be used on the roadside.

Where a sign fails to conform to TSRGD and TSM it is usually fatal to a case where that sign has been contravened. However, s. 85 of the Road Traffic Regulation Act 1984 states that traffic signs for indicating speed restrictions must ensure 'adequate guidance is given to drivers of motor vehicles as to whether, and if so what, limit of speed is to be observed on any road'. Therefore where such 'adequate guidance' is given a conviction may stand even where there are technical breaches of TSRGD and TSM. In *Coombes* v *DPP* [2007] RTR 31 and *DPP* v *Butler* [2010] EWHC 669 (Admin) the courts found that the signs did not conform to the regulations and therefore the speeding convictions were overturned. However in *Peake* v *DPP* [2010] EWHC 286 (Admin) and *Jones* v *DPP* [2011] EWHC 50 (Admin) the courts found that there were 'repeater' signs that provided adequate guidance to motorists and the convictions were ratified despite there being technical faults with some of the signage. That said these cases *cannot* be used by a local authority to counteract their obligations to ensure signage complies with TSRGD and TSM.

Section 81(1) of the 1984 Act states that it shall be unlawful for a person to drive a motor vehicle on a restricted road at a speed exceeding 30 mph.

However, failure by a local authority to erect signs does not amount to a breach of the general statutory duty to maintain highways nor the general duty to promote road safety. As the House of Lords has put it 'drivers [have] to take care for themselves and drive at a safe speed irrespective of whether or not there was a warning sign; they were not entitled to suppose that the need for care on their journeys would be highlighted so as to protect them from their own negligence' (*Gorringe* v *Calderdale MBC* [2004] UKHL 15).

Section 84 allows for speed limits to be imposed on roads other than restricted roads and motorways.

3.7.4.3 Temporary Speed Limits

Section 88 of the 1984 Act provides for both maximum and minimum temporary speed limits to be imposed on certain roads.

Traffic authorities may impose temporary speed *restrictions* in connection with road works or similar operations near to the road which present a danger to the public or serious damage to the highway (see ss. 14 to 16 of the Road Traffic Regulation Act 1984). These restrictions cannot generally exceed 18 months without approval from the Secretary of State.

As *restrictions* rather than speed limits, offences under this heading do not require notices of intended prosecution (*Platten* v *Gowing* [1983] Crim LR 184), neither do they require corroboration.

3.7.4.4 Speed Limits for Particular Classes of Vehicle

The Road Traffic Regulation Act 1984, s. 86 states:

(1) It shall not be lawful for a person to drive a motor vehicle of any class on a road at a speed greater than the speed specified in Schedule 6 to this Act as the maximum speed in relation to a vehicle of that class.
(2) Subject to subsections (4) and (5) below, the Secretary of State may by regulations vary, subject to such conditions as may be specified in the regulations, the provisions of that Schedule.
(3) Regulations under this section may make different provision as respects the same class of vehicles in different circumstances.
(4) …
(5) The Secretary of State shall not have power under this section to vary the speed limit imposed by section 81 of this Act.

3.7.4.5 Exemption for Police, Fire and Ambulance Purposes

The Road Traffic Regulation Act 1984, s. 87 states:

(1) No statutory provision imposing a speed limit on motor vehicles shall apply to any vehicle on an occasion when it is being used for fire and rescue authority, ambulance or police purposes, if the observance of that provision would be likely to hinder the use of the vehicle for the purpose for which it is being used on that occasion.

(1A) Subsection (1) above applies in relation to a vehicle that, although not being used for ambulance purposes, is being used for the purpose of providing a response to an emergency at the request of an NHS ambulance service . . .

(2) Subsection (1) above applies in relation to a vehicle being used—
   (a) for National Crime Agency purposes, or
   (b) for training persons to drive vehicles for use for National Crime Agency purposes, as it applies in relation to a vehicle being used for police purposes.

3.7.4.6 Proof of Speed

Section 89(2) of the 1984 Act requires that a person prosecuted for driving a motor vehicle at a speed exceeding the limit shall not be convicted solely on the evidence of one witness to the effect that, in his/her opinion, the defendant was exceeding the speed limit. Section 88(7) includes a similar provision for failing to attain a minimum speed limit.

The requirements for corroboration do not apply to general speeding offences on motorways (but they do for special classes of vehicle exceeding motorway speed limits).

Corroboration may be provided by the equipment in a police vehicle or by *Vascar* or similar speed measuring equipment (*Nicholas* v *Penny* [1950] 2 KB 466). While it may be preferable, it is not *necessary* in such cases to prove the accuracy of the equipment being used (see e.g. *Darby* v *DPP* [1995] RTR 294).

In *Connell* v *DPP* [2011] EWHC 158 (Admin) the opinion of the police officer was supported by reference to the reading on a Police Pilot device even though the device is an unapproved prescribed device. The magistrates' court allowed the police officer's evidence to be admitted and the High Court upheld the magistrates' court's ruling.

Two police officers may provide sufficient evidence in a case of speeding but the court will decide how much weight to give to such evidence. It is important to show that both officers saw the vehicle at exactly the same time (*Brighty* v *Pearson* [1938] 4 All ER 127).

The signal emitted by a hand-held radar speed gun has been deemed not to amount to a 'communication' for the purposes of the Wireless Telegraphy Act 1949 and a person intercepting such signals cannot be prosecuted under that legislation (*R* v *Crown Court of Knightsbridge, ex parte Foot* [1999] RTR 21).

The Road Traffic Offenders (Prescribed Devices) Order 1999 (SI 1999/162) makes provision for the use of speed cameras that calculate the average speed of a vehicle while passing between two points and allows these readings to be used as proof of the vehicle's speed under s. 20 of the Road Traffic Offenders Act 1988.

The Road Traffic Offenders Act 1988 (s. 20(1)) allows the prosecution to rely on documents such as those produced by prescribed speed detector devices. A condition of the use of such documents is that the document is served on the defendant not less than seven days before trial (s. 20(8)). Where there has been a failure to provide the defendant with a copy of the document, however, the Road Traffic Offenders Act 1988 does not prevent the document being put before the court in the usual way (*DPP* v *Thornley* [2006] EWHC 312 (Admin)).

The heavy reliance on roadside cameras for enforcing speed limits has given rise to some inventive pleading. While it is possible to delay the whole prosecution process for some time by demanding proof of technical and legal data about the cameras, arguing that the driver cannot be ascertained and so forth, such delay is usually simply postponing the inevitable. For an example of the dim view that the courts will take if, having caused many years' delay, a defendant then seeks to rely on that delay as a reason to stay the prosecution see *R (On the Application of Johnson)* v *Stratford Magistrates' Court* [2003] EWHC 353 (QB).

KEYNOTE

In addition to using records from prescribed devices as evidence of speeding offences, s. 20(2) of the Road Traffic Offenders Act 1988 (as amended) allows for evidence from the records of devices (such as ANPR) in relation to driving on the hard shoulder of a motorway and driving through a red X signal to show the closure of a traffic lane.

3.7.4.7 Punishment of Speeding Offences

Speeding offences are punishable under the following Acts:

- Contravening speed limits generally (s. 89(1) of the Road Traffic Regulation Act 1984 and sch. 2 to the Road Traffic Offenders Act 1988).
- Contravening motorway speed limits (other than special classes of vehicle) (s. 17(4) of the Road Traffic Regulation Act 1984 and sch. 2 to the Road Traffic Offenders Act 1988).
- Contravening *minimum* speed limits made under s. 88(1)(b) of the Road Traffic Regulation Act 1984 (s. 88(7) of the Road Traffic Regulation Act 1984 and sch. 2 to the Road Traffic Offenders Act 1988).
- Contravening temporary speed *restrictions* made under s. 14 of the Road Traffic Regulation Act 1984 (s. 16(1) of the Road Traffic Regulation Act 1984 and sch. 2 to the Road Traffic Offenders Act 1988).

The Road Traffic Regulation Act 1984, s. 89(1) states:

(1) A person who drives a motor vehicle on a road at a speed exceeding a limit imposed by or under any enactment to which this section applies shall be guilty of an offence.

3.7.5 Race or Trial of Speed between Vehicles on a Public Way

Sections 12A to 12I of the Road Traffic Act 1988 (as amended by the Deregulation Act 2015) make it an offence to promote or take part in a race or trial of speed between motor vehicles on a public way.

Section 12B allows for a person who wishes to promote a race or trial of speed between motor vehicles on a highway in England and Wales to apply for a permit to a motor sport governing body authorised by regulations. These governing bodies, in England, are the Royal Automobile Club Motor Sports Association Limited and the Auto-Cycle Union Limited.

3.7.6 Causing Danger

OFFENCE: **Causing Danger to Other Road Users—*Road Traffic Act 1988, s. 22A***
- Triable either way • Seven years' imprisonment and/or a fine on indictment
- Six months' imprisonment and/or a fine summarily

The Road Traffic Act 1988, s. 22A states:

(1) A person is guilty of an offence if he intentionally and without lawful authority or reasonable cause—
   (a) causes anything to be on or over a road, or
   (b) interferes with a motor vehicle, trailer or cycle, or
   (c) interferes (directly or indirectly) with traffic equipment,
   in such circumstances that it would be obvious to a reasonable person that to do so would be dangerous.
(2) In subsection (1) above 'dangerous' refers to danger either of injury to any person while on or near a road, or of serious damage to property on or near a road; and in determining for the purposes of that subsection what would be obvious to a reasonable person in a particular case, regard shall be had not only to the circumstances of which he could be expected to be aware but also to any circumstances shown to have been within the knowledge of the accused.
(3) In subsection (1) above 'traffic equipment' means—
   (a) anything lawfully placed on or near a road by a highway authority;
   (b) a traffic sign lawfully placed on or near a road by a person other than a highway authority;
   (c) any fence, barrier or light lawfully placed on or near a road—
      (i) in pursuance of section 174 of the Highways Act 1980, or section 65 of the New Roads and Street Works Act 1991 (which provide for guarding, lighting and signing in streets where works are undertaken), or
      (ii) by a constable or a person acting under the instructions (whether general or specific) of a chief officer of police.
(4) For the purposes of subsection (3) above anything placed on or near a road shall unless the contrary is proved be deemed to have been lawfully placed there.

In assessing whether or not a person has committed the offence under s. 22A(1), the appropriate objective test is 'would a reasonable bystander (whether a motorist or not) consider that the act in question represented an obvious danger?' (*DPP* v *D* [2006] EWHC 314 (Admin)). In the court's view a reasonable person would not expect all motorists to drive carefully and well and should realise that the placing of a traffic sign, for instance, could cause an accident even if the primary factor of such an accident was excessive speed. But note the term 'dangerous' includes a subjective element in that regard will be had to any circumstances shown to be known to the defendant.

A 'road' for the purpose of this offence does not include a footpath (or bridleway) (s. 22A(5)).

This offence is not confined to acts done to the vehicle before it is driven, but also covers interference creating a danger while the vehicle is in the process of being driven. Further, the conduct can take place within the vehicle rather than only external to it, such as dropping objects on to it. In *R* v *Meeking* [2012] EWCA Crim 641 (a case of unlawful act manslaughter), the Court of Appeal held that pulling on the handbrake on a vehicle travelling at 60 mph was an 'unlawful act', contrary to s. 22A.

3.7.6.1 Dangerous Activities on Highways

OFFENCE: **Dangerous Activity on Highways—*Highways Act 1980, ss. 161 to 162***
* Triable summarily * Fine

The Highways Act 1980, ss. 161 to 162 state:

161.—(1) If a person, without lawful authority or excuse, deposits any thing whatsoever on a highway in consequence of which a user of the highway is injured or endangered, that person is guilty of an offence...

    (2) If a person, without lawful authority or excuse—

        (a) lights any fire on or over a highway which consists of or comprises a carriageway; or

        (b) discharges any firearm or firework within [15.24 metres] 50 feet of the centre of such a highway,

    and in consequence a user of the highway is injured, interrupted or endangered, that person is guilty of an offence...

    (3) If a person plays at football or any other game on a highway to the annoyance of a user of the highway he is guilty of an offence...

    (4) If a person, without lawful authority or excuse, allows any filth, dirt, lime or other offensive matter or thing to run or flow on to a highway from any adjoining premises, he is guilty of an offence...

161A.—(1) If a person—

        (a) lights a fire on any land not forming part of a highway which consists of or comprises a carriageway; or

        (b) directs or permits a fire to be lit on any such land,

    and in consequence a user of any highway which consists of or comprises a carriageway is injured, interrupted or endangered by, or by smoke from, that fire or any other fire caused by that fire, that person is guilty of an offence...

162.—A person who for any purpose places any rope, wire or other apparatus across a highway in such a manner as to be likely to cause danger to persons using the highway is, unless he proves that he had taken all necessary means to give adequate warning of the danger, guilty of an offence...

KEYNOTE

'Carriageway' means a way constituting or comprised in a highway, being a way (other than a cycle track) over which the public have a right of way for the passage of vehicles (s. 329 of the 1980 Act).

'Highway' means the whole or part of a highway other than a ferry or waterway and where a highway passed over a bridge or through a tunnel, that bridge or tunnel is to be taken for the purposes of this Act to be part of the highway (s. 328 of the 1980 Act).

The offences at s. 161(1), (2) and (3) and s. 161A(1) are all offences of 'consequence', that is, you must show the relevant consequence (e.g. injury, annoyance, etc.).

Authorised fire-fighters and members of fire and rescue services have powers to stop and regulate traffic and to close highways.

3.7.7 Leaving Vehicles in Dangerous Positions

OFFENCE: **Leaving Vehicles in Dangerous Positions—*Road Traffic Act 1988, s. 22***
- Triable summarily • Fine • Discretionary disqualification

The Road Traffic Act 1988, s. 22 states:

> If a person in charge of a vehicle causes or permits the vehicle or a trailer drawn by it to remain at rest on a road in such a position or in such condition or in such circumstances as to involve a danger of injury to other persons using the road, he is guilty of an offence.

KEYNOTE

This offence involves presenting a danger of injury to other road users by the *position, condition or circumstances* of the vehicle/trailer.

The danger presented by the condition or circumstances of the vehicle is not confined to occasions when it is stationary but will also apply to a vehicle/trailer which presents a danger by moving (such as where a driver fails to set the handbrake (*Maguire* v *Crouch* (1940) 104 JP 445)).

The risk must be to 'other persons using the road'.

3.7.8 Tampering with and Getting on to Vehicles

OFFENCE: **Tampering with Motor Vehicles—*Road Traffic Act 1988, s. 25***
- Triable summarily • Fine

The Road Traffic Act 1988, s. 25 states:

> If, while a motor vehicle is on a road or on a parking place provided by a local authority, a person—
> (a) gets on to the vehicle, or
> (b) tampers with the brake or other part of its mechanism,
> without lawful authority or reasonable cause he is guilty of an offence.

KEYNOTE

This offence, which only applies to 'motor vehicles' and not trailers, can only be committed where the vehicle is on a road or local authority parking place.

What constitutes a part of its mechanism, other than the brake, is open to interpretation but it would appear that anything falling within the ordinary meaning of 'mechanism' would suffice.

If a defendant has got on to or tampered with the vehicle in order to steal it or part of its load, the offence under s. 9 of the Criminal Attempts Act 1981 (interfering) may be appropriate.

OFFENCE: **Holding or Getting on to Vehicle in Motion—*Road Traffic Act 1988, s. 26***
- Triable summarily • Fine

The Road Traffic Act 1988, s. 26 states:

> (1) If, for the purpose of being carried, a person without lawful authority or reasonable cause takes or retains hold of, or gets on to a motor vehicle or trailer while in motion on a road he is guilty of an offence.

(2) If, for the purpose of being drawn, a person takes or retains hold of a motor vehicle or trailer while in motion on a road he is guilty of an offence.

KEYNOTE

For this offence the vehicle or trailer must both be in motion and on a road.

3.7.9 Vehicles Used for Causing Harassment etc.

OFFENCE: **Failing to Stop—*Police Reform Act 2002, s. 59(6)***
- Triable summarily • Fine

The Police Reform Act 2002, s. 59 states:

(1) Where a constable in uniform has reasonable grounds for believing that a motor vehicle is being used on any occasion in a manner which—
   (a) contravenes section 3 or 34 of the Road Traffic Act 1988 (c. 52) (careless and inconsiderate driving and prohibition of off-road driving), and
   (b) is causing, or is likely to cause, alarm, distress or annoyance to members of the public

   he shall have the powers set out in subsection (3).

(2) A constable in uniform shall also have the powers set out in subsection (3) where he has reasonable grounds for believing that a motor vehicle has been used on any occasion in a manner falling within subsection (1).

KEYNOTE

This legislation gives uniformed police officers additional powers to deal with motor vehicles being used in the unlawful, anti-social or just plain annoying ways described.

A point to note here is the definition of a motor vehicle which is *not* that under s. 185 of the Road Traffic Act 1988. For the purposes of these powers above, 'motor vehicle' means any mechanically propelled vehicle *whether or not it is intended or adapted for use on roads* (s. 59(9)). The definition of motor vehicle here will cover everything from go-karts and home-made trials bikes to dumper trucks and building site vehicles.

The constable must be able to point to the existence of *reasonable grounds* giving rise to a belief that the motor vehicle is being or has been used in one of the ways described.

The powers available in these circumstances are listed in s. 59(3):

(a) power, if the motor vehicle is moving, to order the person driving it to stop the vehicle;
(b) power to seize and remove the motor vehicle;
(c) power, for the purposes of exercising a power falling within para. (a) or (b), to enter any premises on which the constable has reasonable grounds for believing the motor vehicle to be;
(d) power to use reasonable force, if necessary, in the exercise of any power conferred by any of paras (a) to (c).

Although the power of entry excludes entry into a 'private dwelling house' (s. 59(7)), that definition *does not include* garages or other structures occupied with the dwelling, nor driveways or other land related to the property (s. 59(9)). This means that the above power is available in relation to garages and driveways of houses.

The powers under s. 59(3) are among those that can be conferred on a Community Support Officer (CSO) designated under sch. 4 to the Police Reform Act 2002. However, a designated CSO cannot enter any premises in the exercise of those powers unless in the company *and* under the supervision of a constable (sch. 4, para. 9(2)).

A vehicle cannot be seized under the s. 59 power unless the officer:

- has warned the person appearing to the officer to be the person whose use falls within subs. (1) that he/she will seize it, if that use continues or is repeated; and
- it appears to the officer that the use has continued or been repeated after the warning (s. 59(4)).

However, a warning is not required if:

- the circumstances make it impracticable for the officer to give a warning;
- the officer has already on that occasion given such a warning in respect of any use of that motor vehicle or of another motor vehicle by that person or any other person;
- the officer has reasonable grounds for believing that such a warning has been given on that occasion otherwise than by him/her; or
- the officer has reasonable grounds for believing that the person whose use of that motor vehicle on that occasion would justify the seizure is a person to whom a warning under that subsection has been given (whether or not by that officer or in respect of the same vehicle or the same or a similar use) on a previous occasion in the previous 12 months (s. 59(5)).

Reference to warning the person 'using' the vehicle here makes the requirements broader than simply warning the relevant *driver*.

The above conditions where a warning will not be needed are alternatives and any one of them will suffice. The sensible provision that a warning is not needed where it would be impracticable to give one is also fairly wide and does not mean the officer has to show it was *impossible* to do so, or even very difficult.

Given the provisions in relation to earlier warnings that may have been given by that or other officers, it will be important from a practical point of view to maintain accurate records of any warnings given.

The Police Reform Act 2002, s. 59 states:

(3) A person who fails to comply with an order under subsection (3)(a) is guilty of an offence . . .

KEYNOTE

The power under s. 59(3)(a) is to order the person *driving* the motor vehicle in the relevant circumstances to stop. 'Driving' has the same meaning as in the Road Traffic Act 1988. If you are going to prosecute someone for failing to comply with the order, you will first need to prove that the order was properly given (e.g. that the person giving it had the authority to do so under the circumstances) and that the order was both heard and understood. The first of those matters will be of particular importance to CSOs. In the context of the general power to stop vehicles on roads, 'stop' has been held to mean bringing the vehicle to a halt and remaining at rest long enough for the officer to exercise whatever additional powers are appropriate (*Lodwick* v *Sanders* [1985] 1 WLR 382). If the same interpretation is given to the power here, 'stopping' must be at least long enough to allow the officer to deliver the statutory warning if appropriate, or perhaps to check whether any such warning has already been given. Although the power does not extend to demanding the keys from the driver, the section clearly gives uniformed officers powers of enforcement, including a power to use reasonable force if necessary.

The Police (Retention and Disposal of Motor Vehicles) Regulations 2002 (SI 2002/3049) (as amended) provide detailed regulation over the seizing and retention of vehicles under the above power, including the steps which must be taken to serve seizure notices and the time limits for doing so.

Under reg. 4, the relevant authority having custody of the vehicle must take steps to give a notice to the person who owns the vehicle. The date specified in the seizure notice, on or before which the person must claim the vehicle, must be a date not less than seven working days from the day on which the notice was given to that person (reg. 4). The notice must indicate that charges may be payable by that person and that the vehicle may be retained until these charges are paid. The level of the charges is set out in reg. 6.

If, before a vehicle is disposed of by an authority, a person satisfies the authority that he/she is the owner and pays the relevant fee in respect of its removal and retention, the authority must permit that person to remove the vehicle (reg. 5).

If a person can prove that:

- the use of the vehicle causing it to be seized under s. 59 was not a use by that person;
- he/she did not know of the use of the vehicle in the manner which led to its seizure; and
- he/she had not consented to its use in that manner and could not, by the taking of reasonable steps, have prevented its use in that manner,

no charge is payable by that person (reg. 5(3)).

Where the authority is unable to serve a notice on the owner of the vehicle, or that person fails to remove the vehicle from its custody, the authority must take further steps to identify the owner of the vehicle. Where the person appearing to be the owner of the vehicle fails to comply with a seizure notice under reg. 4(1) or where the authority has not been able, having taken such steps as are reasonably practicable, to give a seizure notice to that person, the relevant authority can (subject to the time limits specified) dispose of the vehicle (reg. 7). Where a vehicle is sold, the net proceeds of sale are payable to the owner of a vehicle, if he/she makes a claim within a year of the sale (reg. 8).

3.7.10 Smoking in Vehicles

It is illegal to smoke in a car (or other vehicle) with anyone under 18. The law changed to protect children and young people from the dangers of second-hand smoke.

The Smoke-free (Private Vehicles) Regulations 2015 (SI 2015/286) amended the Smoke-free (Exemptions and Vehicles) Regulations 2007 (SI 2007/765) and designated all road vehicles that were not already covered by that existing smoke-free legislation as smoke-free places, when a person under 18 is present in the vehicle.

Regulation 11(1A) of the Smoke-free (Exemptions and Vehicles) Regulations 2007 states:

A vehicle that is not smoke-free by virtue of paragraph (1), or any part of such a vehicle, is smoke-free if—
(a) it is enclosed,
(b) there is more than one person present in the vehicle, and
(c) a person under the age of 18 is present in the vehicle.

KEYNOTE

Drivers and passengers who break the law could face a penalty fine of £50. The law applies to every driver in England and Wales, including those aged 17 and those with a provisional driving licence.

The law applies:

- to any private vehicle that is enclosed wholly or partly by a roof;
- when people have the windows or sunroof open, or the air conditioning on;
- when someone sits smoking in the open doorway of a vehicle.

The law does not apply to:

- e-cigarettes (vaping);
- a driver who is 17 years old if they are on their own in the car;
- a convertible car with the roof completely down.

Caravans and motor caravans are also excluded when they are being used as living accommodation.

3.7.11 Shining or Directing a Laser Beam Towards a Vehicle

OFFENCE: **Offence of Shining or Directing a Laser Beam Towards a Vehicle—**
The Laser Misuse (Vehicles) Act 2018, s. 1
- Triable either way • Five years' imprisonment and/or a fine on indictment
- 12 months' imprisonment and/or a fine summarily

The Laser Misuse (Vehicles) Act 2018, s. 1 states:

(1) A person commits an offence if—
(a) the person shines or directs a laser beam towards a vehicle which is moving or ready to move, and
(b) the laser beam dazzles or distracts, or is likely to dazzle or distract, a person with control of the vehicle…

KEYNOTE

This legislation is a response to concerns expressed over the years, particularly in the aviation industry, about laser pens being shone in the direction of aircraft, threatening the safety of the craft and the eyesight of pilots and other personnel. However, it is extended to 'vehicles'. In this legislation 'vehicle' means any vehicle used for travel by land, water or air (s. 3). By virtue of s. 1(6) a mechanically propelled vehicle which is not moving or ready to move but whose engine or motor is running is to be treated for the purposes of subs. (1)(a) as ready to move.

There is a defence to show that the person had a reasonable excuse for shining or directing the laser beam towards the vehicle, or that the person:

- did not intend to shine or direct the laser beam towards the vehicle; and
- exercised all due diligence and took all reasonable precautions to avoid doing so.

3.8 | Construction and Use

3.8.1 Introduction

The law governing the construction and use of road vehicles is mainly to be found—as the name suggests—in the Road Vehicles (Construction and Use) Regulations 1986 (SI 1986/1078). The Regulations deal with everything from motor cycle sidestands (reg. 38) to the placing of mascots (reg. 53). These Regulations are frequently amended as the law develops.

3.8.2 The Road Vehicles (Construction and Use) Regulations 1986

Many of the principal rules relating to the use of vehicles on roads are to be found in the Road Vehicles (Construction and Use) Regulations 1986. Some of the offences are aimed at the driving or control of the vehicle but most are concerned with the condition of the vehicle, its equipment and specifications.

Regulation 3 sets out the relevant definitions; where there is no specific definition, those used under the Road Traffic Act 1988 will usually apply.

In bringing a prosecution for an offence under these Regulations it is important to establish whether the correct offence is 'using', 'causing' or 'permitting'. It is also important to establish whether a particular regulation applies to vehicles *first used* on or after a certain date; *first registered* on or after a certain date; or *manufactured* on or after a certain date. In addition to the general condition and use of the relevant vehicle, the regulations can require the fitting of specific equipment to vehicles. For example, certain vehicles such as those with eight or more passenger seats are (or will be) required to have 'speed limiters'.

Certain vehicles are exempted from the Regulations (reg. 4).

3.8.2.1 Brakes

Regulations 15 to 19 set out the requirements as to braking systems on vehicles, together with those for their maintenance. It is not absolutely *necessary* for the person testing the braking system of a vehicle to be a 'qualified examiner' (see *Stoneley* v *Richardson* [1973] RTR 229 where a constable testified to being able to push the defendant's car along with the handbrake applied).

The offence of breaching the requirement in relation to brakes is prosecuted under s. 41A of the Road Traffic Act 1988.

See also s. 75 of the Road Traffic Act 1988 for the offence of selling unroadworthy vehicles.

3.8.2.2 Steering Gear

Regulation 29 states that all steering gear fitted to a motor vehicle shall at all times while the vehicle is used on a road be maintained in good and efficient working order and be properly adjusted.

3.8.2.3 Tyres

Section 41A of the 1988 Act also applies where the requirements in relation to tyres have been breached.

Regulation 24 sets out the requirements as to what tyres must be fitted to which vehicles, while reg. 25 restricts the speed limits and loads for such vehicles. Regulation 26 generally prohibits the mixing of different types of tyre (e.g. diagonal ply, bias-belted or radial ply) on both the same axle or different axles (although some combination is permissible). Regulation 27 sets out a number of specific defects that will make tyres unlawful. It also contains exemptions for certain vehicles. The defects, in reg. 27(1), are where:

(a) the tyre is unsuitable having regard to the use to which the motor vehicle or trailer is being put or to the types of tyres fitted to its other wheels;

(b) the tyre is not so inflated as to make it fit for the use to which the motor vehicle or trailer is being put;

(c) the tyre has a cut in excess of 25mm or 10% of the section width of the tyre, whichever is the greater, measured in any direction on the outside of the tyre and deep enough to reach the ply or cord;

(d) the tyre has any lump, bulge or tear caused by separation or partial failure of its structure;

(e) the tyre has any of the ply or cord exposed;

(f) the base of any groove which showed in the original tread pattern of the tyre is not clearly visible;

(g) either—

  (i) the grooves of the tread pattern of the tyre do not have a depth of at least 1 mm throughout a continuous band measuring at least three-quarters of the breadth of the tread and round the entire outer circumference of the tyre; or

  (ii) if the grooves of the original tread pattern of the tyre did not extend beyond three-quarters of the breadth of the tread, any groove which showed in the original tread pattern does not have a depth of at least 1mm; or

(h) the tyre is not maintained in such condition as to be fit for the use to which the vehicle or trailer is being put or has a defect which might in any way cause damage to the surface of the road or damage to persons on or in the vehicle or to other persons using the road.

Regulation 27 also places restrictions on 'recut' tyres (reg. 27(5)) and provides for many exemptions from the above conditions.

KEYNOTE

The use on roads of some 'knobbly' tyres or others which are designed for off-road use (on vehicles such as quad-bikes) may be prosecuted under reg. 27(1)(a) if it can be shown that the tyres were 'unsuitable having regard to the use to which the vehicle was put'.

To avoid the defect at reg. 27(1)(b) the tyre must be inflated so as to make it fit for the use to which the vehicle is being put at the material time; it does not have to be so inflated as to make it fit for some future use, however probable that use might be (*Connor* v *Graham* [1981] RTR 291).

In the case of:

- 'passenger vehicles other than motor cycles constructed or adapted to carry no more than eight seated passengers in addition to the driver' (a 'passenger vehicle' is a vehicle constructed solely for the carriage of passengers and their effects),

- 'goods vehicles with a maximum gross weight which does not exceed 3500 kg' (a 'goods vehicle' is a motor vehicle or trailer constructed or adapted for use for the carriage or haulage of goods or burden of any description),

- 'light trailers'

(first used on or after 3 January 1933 in each case) the depth of tread requirement is increased to 1.6 mm throughout a continuous band across the central 3/4 section of the tyre and around the entire circumference. For these three types of vehicle paras 27(1)(f) and (g) shall not apply.

The entire outer circumference of a tyre does not usually include the outer walls or shoulder as they are not in contact with road (*Coote* v *Parkin* [1977] RTR 61).

'Tread pattern' includes plain surfaces as well as cut grooves but it does *not* cover tie-bars and tread wear indicators as used on the tyres of many goods and heavy vehicles.

Evidence as to the defective condition of a tyre may be given by anyone who saw it and it is no defence to argue that the tyre was not examined by an authorised vehicle examiner (*Phillips* v *Thomas* [1974] RTR 28).

Exemptions

Regulation 27(4) sets out a number of exemptions to the provisions at (a)–(g) above, the main ones being:

- agricultural motor vehicles driven at not more than 20 mph
- agricultural trailers
- broken down vehicles or vehicles proceeding to a place to be broken up, being drawn in either case, by a motor vehicle at not more than 20 mph.

The onus appears to be on defendants to show that their vehicle falls into an exempted category and that burden is not discharged simply by showing that the vehicle's excise licence describes it as being in one such category (*Wakeman* v *Catlow* [1977] RTR 174).

3.8.2.4 Breach of Requirement: Brakes, Steering Gear or Tyres

OFFENCE: **Breach of Requirement: Brakes, Steering Gear or Tyres—*Road Traffic Act 1988, s. 41A***

- Triable summarily • Fine • Discretionary disqualification under specified conditions

The Road Traffic Act 1988, s. 41A states:

A person who—
    (a) contravenes or fails to comply with a construction and use requirement as to brakes, steering-gear or tyres, or
    (b) uses on a road a motor vehicle or trailer which does not comply with such a requirement, or causes or permits a motor vehicle or trailer to be so used,
    is guilty of an offence.

3.8.2.5 Weights

The weight of a vehicle will often determine its classification and the use to which it may be put, together with the licensing conditions of those who drive it.

Reference will usually be made to the laden weight or the gross weight of a vehicle in offences involving its construction and use. For construction and use purposes, the gross weight under reg. 3(2) of the 1986 Regulations will be:

- For motor vehicles—the sum of the weights transmitted to the road surface by all its wheels.
- For trailers—the sum of the weights transmitted to the road surface by all its wheels *and* of any weight of the trailer which is imposed on the drawing vehicle.
- *Axle* weights are, generally, the sum of the weights transmitted to the road surface by all the wheels of that axle.

Offences concerning the speed and excise duty of larger vehicles will usually be concerned with laden and unladen weight. Calculation of a vehicle's unladen weight for most purposes is contained under s. 190 of the Road Traffic Act 1988.

Most locomotives, motor tractors and heavy motor cars are required to show their unladen weight, either on their nearside or on the relevant plating certificate(s).

OFFENCE: **Breach of Weight Requirements—Goods and Passenger Vehicles—**
Road Traffic Act 1988, s. 41B

• Triable summarily • Fine

The Road Traffic Act 1988, s. 41B states:

(1) A person who—
  (a) contravenes or fails to comply with a construction and use requirement as to any description of weight applicable to—
    (i) a goods vehicle, or
    (ii) a motor vehicle or trailer adapted to carry more than eight passengers, or
  (b) uses on a road a vehicle which does not comply with such a requirement, or causes or permits a vehicle to be so used,
  is guilty of an offence.

KEYNOTE

The definitions of a 'goods vehicle' and a 'passenger vehicle' are given at **para. 3.8.2.3, Keynote.**

Defence

The Road Traffic Act 1988, s. 41B states:

(2) In any proceedings for an offence under this section in which there is alleged a contravention of or failure to comply with a construction and use requirement as to any description of weight applicable to a goods vehicle, it shall be a defence to prove either—
  (a) that at the time when the vehicle was being used on the road—
    (i) it was proceeding to a weighbridge which was the nearest available one to the place where the loading of the vehicle was completed for the purpose of being weighed, or
    (ii) it was proceeding from a weighbridge after being weighed to the nearest point at which it was reasonably practicable to reduce the weight to the relevant limit, without causing an obstruction on any road, or
  (b) in a case where the limit of that weight was not exceeded by more than 5 per cent—
    (i) that that limit was not exceeded at the time when the loading of the vehicle was originally completed, and
    (ii) that since that time no person has made any addition to the load.

3.8.2.6 Mobile Phones

Regulation 110 sets out a variety of prohibitions on the use of hand-held mobile phones and devices. Contravening this regulation will mean an offence under s. 41D of the Road Traffic Act 1988 has been committed.

The Road Vehicles (Construction and Use) Regulations 1986, reg. 110 states:

(1) No person shall drive a motor vehicle on a road if he is using—
  (a) a hand-held mobile telephone; or
  (b) a hand-held device of a kind specified in paragraph (4).
(2) No person shall cause or permit any other person to drive a motor vehicle on a road while that other person is using—
  (a) a hand-held mobile telephone; or
  (b) a hand-held device of a kind specified in paragraph (4).
(3) No person shall supervise a holder of a provisional licence if the person supervising is using—
  (a) a hand-held mobile telephone; or
  (b) a hand-held device of a kind specified in paragraph (4),
  at a time when the provisional licence holder is driving a motor vehicle on a road.
(4) A device referred to in paragraphs (1)(b), (2)(B) and (3)(b) is a device, other than a two-way radio, which performs an interactive communication function by transmitting and receiving data.

• Triable summarily • Fine • Discretionary disqualification • Obligatory endorsement—three points

The Road Traffic Act 1988, s. 41D states:

A person who contravenes or fails to comply with a construction and use requirement—

(a) as to not driving a motor vehicle in a position which does not give proper control or a full view of the road and traffic ahead, or not causing or permitting the driving of a motor vehicle by another person in such a position, or

(b) as to not driving or supervising the driving of a motor vehicle while using a hand-held mobile telephone or other hand-held interactive communication device, or not causing or permitting the driving of a motor vehicle by another person using such a telephone or other device,

is guilty of an offence.

KEYNOTE

A hand-held device is something that 'is or must be held at some point during the course of making or receiving a call or performing any other interactive communication function'. The offence applies if a phone has to be 'held' while making or receiving a call. 'Cradling' a phone by wedging the phone between the ear and shoulder—or anywhere else—constitutes 'holding' a phone. Even the use of some hands-free attachments or earpieces may still amount to offences under this legislation.

The penalty fine for using a mobile phone is now £200 and 6 penalty points; this means new drivers will have their licences revoked for one offence. There is also no opportunity for a driver remedial course.

'Interactive communication function' includes the sending and receiving of oral or written messages, faxes, still or moving images and access to the internet (reg. 110(6)(c)). Therefore it covers text messages and photographs sent or received by mobile phones.

In *Attorney-General's Reference (No. 17 of 2009)* [2009] EWCA Crim 1003, the Court of Appeal confirmed that there is never any excuse for texting or using a hand-held mobile phone while driving. However, the regulations provide for a specific defence under very limited circumstances. These circumstances are where the person:

• is using the telephone or other device to call the police, fire, ambulance or other emergency service on 112 or 999;

• is acting in response to a genuine emergency; and

• it is unsafe or impracticable for the person to cease driving in order to make the call (or, in the case of the third offence, for the provisional licence holder to cease driving while the call was being made).

(reg. 110(5))

All three features must be present if the defence is to apply.

Note that the Road Vehicles (Construction and Use) (Amendment) Regulations 2018 allow an exemption to permit use of a hand-held mobile telephone or hand-held device to perform a remote-control parking manoeuvre.

Even if a driver or supervisor is complying with the specific regulations regarding the use of mobile phones and devices he/she may still have impaired control of the vehicle and therefore commit the other offences referred to. As the Highway Code puts it:

You MUST exercise proper control of your vehicle at all times. Never use a hand held mobile phone or microphone when driving. Using hands free equipment is also likely to distract your attention from the road. It is far safer not to use any telephone while you are driving—find a safe place to stop first.

3.8.2.7 Exhaust Systems and Audible Warning Instruments

Regulations 54 and 57 regulate the fitting and use of silencers. The regulations provide that every vehicle propelled by an internal combustion engine shall be fitted with an exhaust system including a silencer and the exhaust gases from the engine shall not escape into the atmosphere without passing through the silencer and exhaust system. The silencer shall be maintained in good and efficient working order and shall not be altered so as to increase the noise made by the escape of exhaust gases.

Regulations 37 and 99 regulate the fitting and use of audible warning instruments. Every motor vehicle which has a maximum speed of more than 20 mph shall be fitted with a horn, not being a reversing alarm or a two-tone horn. This does not apply to an agricultural motor vehicle, unless it is being driven at more than 20 mph. The sound emitted by any horn, other than a reversing alarm, boarding aid alarm or a two-tone horn, fitted to a wheeled vehicle first used on or after 1 August 1973, shall be continuous, uniform and not loud or harsh. A general prohibition on the use of an audible warning instrument while the vehicle is stationary on a road (except to warn of danger) is made by reg. 99, which also prohibits the use of such instruments between 11.30 pm and 7 am on a restricted road.

Generally, no motor vehicle shall be fitted with a bell, gong, siren or two-tone horn but a bell, gong or siren may be fitted to prevent theft or attempted theft of the motor vehicle or its contents and also to a bus to summon help for the driver, conductor or an inspector. If the device is fitted to prevent theft and the vehicle was first used on or after 1 October 1982, another device must be fitted so as to stop the bell, gong or siren after it has sounded continuously for more than five minutes. Every such device shall be maintained in good working order.

As an exception to the general rule, a bell, gong, siren or two-tone horn may be fitted to a vehicle, examples of which include:

- if used for fire brigade, ambulance or police purposes;
- if used by a body formed primarily for the purposes of fire salvage and used for those or similar purposes;
- if used by the Forestry Commission or local authority for fighting fires;
- if used for bomb disposal;
- if used by the blood transfusion service;
- if used as a Coastguard vehicle;
- if used for mine rescue;
- if used by the RAF mountain rescue service;
- if used by the Royal National Lifeboat Institute for the purpose of launching lifeboats;
- if used for mountain rescue purposes.

3.8.2.8 Breach of Construction and Use Requirements

OFFENCE: **Breach of Other Construction and Use Requirements—*Road Traffic Act 1988, s. 42***

- Triable summarily • Fine

The Road Traffic Act 1988, s. 42 states:

A person who—
(a) contravenes or fails to comply with any construction or use requirement other than one within section 41A(a) or 41B(1)(a) or 41D of this Act, or
(b) uses on a road a motor vehicle or trailer which does not comply with such a requirement, or causes or permits a motor vehicle or trailer to be so used,
is guilty of an offence.

KEYNOTE

Under s. 44 of the Act the Secretary of State may make regulations allowing road use by vehicles that would otherwise contravene the above sections. Such vehicles are usually of extraordinary dimensions such as construction equipment or vehicles for moving abnormal indivisible loads.

3.8.2.9 Dangerous Use or Condition

Regulation 100 contains a catch-all provision to prevent the use of vehicles in a way which presents a danger to others. There are many ways in which that danger can be brought about (e.g. insecure loading, using the vehicle in a way which causes a nuisance, having the vehicle in a poor general condition). This regulation, which would apply to vehicles carrying too many people or vehicles being used for an unsuitable purpose, overlaps to a large extent with the offences under ss. 22A (causing danger to other road users) and 40A (using vehicles in a dangerous condition) of the Road Traffic Act 1988.

OFFENCE: **Using a Vehicle in Dangerous Condition etc.—*Road Traffic Act 1988, s. 40A***
- Triable summarily • Fine • Obligatory disqualification if committed within three years of a previous conviction of the offender under s. 40A. Discretionary disqualification in any other case

The Road Traffic Act 1988, s. 40A states:

A person is guilty of an offence if he uses, or causes or permits another to use, a motor vehicle or trailer on a road when—
- (a) the condition of the motor vehicle or trailer, or of its accessories or equipment, or
- (b) the purpose for which it is used, or
- (c) the number of passengers carried by it, or the manner in which they are carried, or
- (d) the weight, position or distribution of its load, or the manner in which it is secured,

is such that the use of the motor vehicle or trailer involves a danger of injury to any person.

KEYNOTE

Section 40A creates an offence of:

- using, causing or permitting another to use
- on a road
- a motor vehicle or trailer
- which, for whatever reason, involves a danger of injury
- to any person.

The existence of any danger is a question of fact, although s. 40A has to be read in conjunction with reg. 100(1) of the Road Vehicles (Construction and Use) Regulations 1986 (*DPP* v *Potts* [2000] RTR 1).

The test in relation to the potential for injury is an objective one and will consider the anticipated eventualities of the ordinary course of driving including the need for sudden braking, swerving, etc. (*Akelis* v *Normand* 1997 SLT 136). For example, in *Gray* v *DPP* [1999] RTR 339, a seven-year-old boy was seen to be travelling in the open back of an uncovered jeep without any fitted restraints. The boy was steadying himself by holding on to the vehicle's roll-bars. The court held that, even though he had travelled in that way without incident many times in the past, and his father, the driver, was generally a responsible parent, the objective test as to the potential for injury meant that the offence (under s. 40A(c)) had been committed.

3.8.3 Lights

The law which governs the fitting and use of lights on vehicles is to be found in the Road Vehicles Lighting Regulations 1989 (SI 1989/1796). They are made under s. 41 of the Road Traffic Act 1988, for all vehicles except cycles (which are made under s. 81).

The main lights are themselves divided into several groups including:

- headlamps (main beam and dipped)
- front and rear position lamps (side lights)

Also included in the 1989 Regulations are reflectors and markers.

3.8.3.1 Definitions

Regulation 3 sets out the definitions for the purposes of the 1989 Regulations. Again, where none is specified, the corresponding definition under the Road Traffic Act 1988 will usually apply.

The Regulations separate a 24-hour period into:

- the period between sunset and sunrise
- the period between sunrise and sunset.

Where the old distinction of 'daytime hours' and 'hours of darkness' applies, reg. 3 defines them as 'the time between half an hour before sunrise and half an hour after sunset' and 'the time between half an hour after sunset and half an hour before sunrise' respectively.

3.8.3.2 Exemptions

Regulations 4 to 9A list the exemptions which include:

4. ...
(3) Nothing in these Regulations shall require any lamp or reflector to be fitted between sunrise and sunset to—
    (a) a vehicle not fitted with any front or rear position lamp,
    (b) an incomplete vehicle proceeding to a works for completion,
    (c) a pedal cycle,
    (d) a pedestrian-controlled vehicle,
    (e) a horse-drawn vehicle,
    (f) a vehicle drawn or propelled by hand, or
    (g) a combat vehicle.
5. Temporarily imported vehicles and vehicles proceeding to a port for export
6. Vehicles towing or being towed
7. Military vehicles
8. Invalid carriages
9. Vehicles drawn or propelled by hand
9A. Tram cars.

Other exemptions will apply to some parked vehicles (see e.g. reg. 24).

An important class of exempt vehicles is 'emergency vehicles'. These are defined in reg. 3 and include the usual emergency services vehicles (police, ambulance, fire) and also in some cases (e.g. use of blue lights) vehicles used by other agencies such as HM Revenue & Customs and the Ministry of Defence.

3.8.3.3 Offences

Offences contravening the lighting regulations are charged under s. 41 of the Road Traffic Act 1988 in the same ways as the other construction and use offences above.

3.8.4 Testing

Section 47 of the Road Traffic Act 1988 requires all motor vehicles which were first registered more than three years before the time when they are being used on a road to pass a test (MOT test). That requirement includes vehicles manufactured abroad (s. 47(2)(b)). Since May 2018 vehicles will not need an MOT from the 40th anniversary of when they were registered or manufactured.

Some vehicles need to be tested after one year, notably:

- motor vehicles having more than eight seats (excluding the driver's seat) which are used to carry passengers
- taxis
- ambulances.

The procedure for testing of vehicles is set out in the Motor Vehicles (Tests) Regulations 1981, as amended. These and their many amending Regulations lay down both the instructions for carrying out a test and also specify those items which will be tested.

Tests can only be carried out by 'authorised examiners' and others listed in s. 45(3) and vehicle examiners appointed under s. 66A (as amended by the Road Traffic (Vehicle Testing) Act 1999). Many garages are so authorised. Roadside tests may also be carried out in some circumstances.

Where a garage returned a car to its owner on the understanding that it had been repaired and had passed its MOT when in fact it was unroadworthy, the garage was held to have committed the offence of 'supplying' an unroadworthy vehicle contrary to s. 75 of the Road Traffic Act 1988 (*Devon County Council* v *DB Cars* [2001] EWHC Admin 521). In that case the High Court held that the word 'supply' involved no more than a transfer of physical control of an item from one person to another in order to provide the other person with something that he/she wanted. As the garage owner transferred physical control of the car to the owner he had, on that definition, 'supplied' it.

The test will categorise defects and faults under three categories: Dangerous, Minor and Major. These categories grade the severity and danger of a fault.

Minor faults may still pass the test, but they will be flagged up on the MoT certificate alongside advisory notice.

OFFENCE: **Using, Causing or Permitting Use of Vehicle without Test Certificate— Road Traffic Act 1988, s. 47(1)**
- Triable summarily • Fine

The Road Traffic Act 1988, s. 47 states:

(1) A person who uses on a road at any time, or causes or permits to be so used, a motor vehicle to which this section applies, and as respects which no test certificate has been issued within the appropriate period before that time, is guilty of an offence.

In this section and s. 48 of this Act, the 'appropriate period' means a period of 12 months or such shorter period as may be prescribed.

KEYNOTE

Where someone applies for a vehicle excise licence (under the Vehicle Excise and Registration Act 1994):

- the person applying must provide an effective test certificate for the vehicle, or
- show from records maintained under s. 45(6B) of the 1988 Act evidence that such a test certificate has been granted, or
- make a declaration in the specified form.

Alternatively, in the case of an exempt vehicle (see below) the owner of the vehicle can declare in writing the year in which the vehicle was manufactured, and that the period of three years from the date of manufacture has not expired (Motor Vehicles (Evidence of Test Certificates) Regulations 2004 (SI 2004/1896)).

As ever, there are numerous exemptions to the requirements of s. 47, most of which relate to larger vehicles, track-laying vehicles and some pedestrian-controlled vehicles (reg. 6 of the 1981 Regulations). Some military vehicles, some electrically-powered goods vehicles and vehicles temporarily in Great Britain are also exempt.

Vehicles *provided* (as opposed to 'used') for police purposes are exempt if they are maintained in an approved police workshop (reg. 6(1)(xiv)). Other exemptions exist in relation to vehicles seized or detained by the police or customs and excise officers.

Special provision is made (under s. 48) for the issue of temporary exemption certificates in the case of certain public service vehicles. Vehicles manufactured before 1 January 1960 are also exempt from the requirement (Motor Vehicles (Tests) (Amendment) (No. 2) Regulations 2012 (SI 2012/2652)).

An exemption exists where the person using the vehicle is taking it to or from a testing centre. This exemption is only applicable where the test has been previously arranged with the garage. A further exemption exists where a test certificate has been refused and the vehicle is:

- being delivered by prior arrangement, or brought from the place where the relevant work is to be/has been carried out; or
- being towed to a place where it is to be broken up.

Provision is made in reg. 6 for the use of a vehicle by an authorised examiner or inspector during the test.

3.8.4.1 Roadside Tests

Section 67 of the Road Traffic Act 1988 allows 'authorised examiners' to carry out roadside tests on motor vehicles, in relation to the brakes, steering, tyres, lights and noise and fume emission. Authorised examiners include police constables so authorised by their chief officer of police. Other examiners may be appointed (e.g. by the Secretary of State or a police authority) but they must produce their authority to act as such if required to do so (s. 67(5)). Obstructing such an examiner is a summary offence under s. 67(9).

The Road Vehicles (Powers to Stop) Regulations 2011 (SI 2011/996) enables the appointment of uniformed stopping officers with powers to stop vehicles on roads for a number of purposes.

The Road Traffic Act 1988, s. 66C states:

(1) A person commits an offence if the person, with intent to deceive, impersonates a stopping officer or makes any statement or does any act calculated falsely to suggest that the person is a stopping officer.

(2) A person commits an offence if the person resists or wilfully obstructs a stopping officer who is exercising the powers of a stopping officer.

Section 67(6) allows for drivers to ask for the examination to be deferred (in accordance with the time limits set out at sch. 2 to the 1988 Act). However, s. 67 goes on to state:

(7) Where it appears to—
   (a) a constable, or
   (b) in the case of a vehicle to which subsection (3B) applies, a stopping officer, that, by reason of an accident having occurred owing to the presence of the vehicle on a road, it is requisite that a test should be carried out forthwith, the constable or stopping officer may require it to be so carried out and, if the constable or stopping officer is not to carry it out himself, may require that the vehicle shall not be taken away until the test has been carried out.

(8) Where in the opinion of—
   (a) a constable, or
   (b) in the case of a vehicle to which subsection (3B) applies, a stopping officer, the vehicle is apparently so defective that it ought not to be allowed to proceed without a test being carried out, the constable or stopping officer may require the test to be carried out forthwith.

(9) If a person obstructs an authorised examiner acting under this section, or fails to comply with a requirement of this section or Schedule 2 to this Act, he is guilty of an offence.

(10) In this section and in Schedule 2 to this Act—
   (a) 'test' includes 'inspect' or 'inspection', as the case may require, and
   (b) references to a vehicle include references to a trailer drawn by it.

3.8.4.2 Testing and Inspection

Regulation 74 of the Road Vehicles (Construction and Use) Regulations 1986 provides a power to test and inspect the:

- brakes
- silencers
- steering gear
- tyres

of any vehicle on any premises where that vehicle is located.

The power applies to police officers in uniform and other authorised vehicle examiners (see reg. 74(1)(a)–(f)). Regulation 74 does provide a power of entry, however. It also provides that no such test or inspection shall be carried out unless:

- the owner of the vehicle consents;
- notice has been given to that owner (either personally or left at his/her address not less than 48 hours before the time of the proposed test/inspection, or sent to him/her by recorded delivery at least 72 hours before the proposed test/inspection); or
- the test or inspection is made within 48 hours of a reportable accident in which the vehicle was involved.

3.9 | Driver Licensing

This chapter is only tested in the Sergeants' examination—Inspectors' examination candidates should not study this material.

3.9.1 | Introduction

The law regulating driver licensing is governed primarily by the Motor Vehicles (Driving Licences) Regulations 1999 (SI 1999/2864).

Most of the relevant legislation governing the licensing of drivers to drive motor vehicles can be found in the 1999 Regulations, together with:

- Part III of the Road Traffic Act 1988
- The Road Traffic (Driver Licensing and Information Systems) Act 1989
- The Road Traffic (New Drivers) Act 1995.

The 1999 Regulations should be consulted when considering offences or entitlements to drive. Infringement is generally charged under the Road Traffic Offenders Act 1988, s. 91.

3.9.2 | The Licence

A driving licence must be issued in the form prescribed by the Secretary of State under s. 98 of the Road Traffic Act 1988. The photocard driving licence was introduced in 1998 as part of the harmonisation process between our domestic road traffic legislation and that of the rest of the European Union (see the Driving Licences (Community Driving Licence) Regulations 1998 (SI 1998/1420)).

Photocard licences are *pink* for full licence holders and *green* for provisional licence holders. Licences held by drivers in Wales are printed in both Welsh and English.

Photocard licences are the same size as a credit card and contain the holder's:

- name
- address
- date of birth
- driver number
- driving entitlement
- photograph
- electronically copied signature
- information codes showing any restrictions that apply to the holder.

They can be of particular practical importance and will indicate, for instance, whether the driver is supposed to be wearing spectacles or some other form of visual correction.

Licence holders must surrender their licence to the Secretary of State on changing name or address and failure to do so is a summary offence under s. 99(5) of the Road Traffic Act 1988. The Secretary of State may also revoke driving licences under certain conditions (see e.g. s. 93 of the 1988 Act).

Regulation 4 of the Motor Vehicles (Driving Licences) (Amendment) (No. 3) Regulations 2015 (SI 2015/719) prohibits a person from holding more than one British, Northern Ireland or Community driving licence.

| 3.9.2.1 | **Expiry of Licences** |

The photocard licence is renewable every 10 years, and a reminder, with the appropriate form, is sent by the DVLA to the address on its records.

Licences will *generally* last until the holder's 70th birthday or for three years, whichever is the longer (s. 99 of the Road Traffic Act 1988). On reaching 70, drivers may renew their licence every three years. This applies to full driving licences and most provisional licences.

Large goods vehicles and passenger carrying vehicles licences last until the driver's 45th birthday or five years, whichever is the longer. If the driver is between 45 and 65 they last for five years or until the holder's 66th birthday, whichever is the shorter. After the driver has reached 65 the licence must be renewed annually.

A large goods vehicle (LGV) is defined under s. 121 of the Road Traffic Act 1988 as:

- a motor vehicle (not being a medium-sized goods vehicle)
- which is constructed or adapted
- to carry or haul goods
- having a permissible maximum weight over 7.5 tonnes.

A passenger-carrying vehicle (PCV) is defined under s. 121 as either:

- a vehicle used for carrying passengers
- which is constructed or adapted
- to carry more than 16 passengers (a 'large PCV')

or

- a vehicle used for carrying passengers *for hire or reward*
- which is constructed or adapted
- to carry more than 8 but not more than 16 passengers (a 'small PCV').

Provisional licences for motor cycles remain generally valid until the holder's 70th birthday (reg. 15 as amended by the Motor Vehicles (Driving Licences) (Amendment) Regulations 2001 (SI 2001/53)).

| 3.9.2.2 | **Failure to Provide Signature or Sign Licence on Receipt** |

It is a summary offence (under reg. 20 of the Motor Vehicles (Driving Licences) Regulations 1999 and s. 91 of the Road Traffic Offenders Act 1988) to fail to sign a driving licence in ink as soon as it is received by the holder. Holders of the photocard licence are required to provide a signature on the relevant form in order that the DVLA can reproduce their signature electronically on that photocard and both failures are provided for under the wording of reg. 20.

| 3.9.3 | **Learner Drivers** |

Learner drivers are generally required to hold provisional licences. The granting of provisional licences is governed by s. 97(3) of the Road Traffic Act 1988 which states:

(3) A provisional licence—
    (a) shall be granted subject to prescribed conditions,
    (b) shall, in any cases prescribed for the purposes of this paragraph, be restricted so as to author-ise only the driving of vehicles of the classes so prescribed,
    (c) may, in the case of a person appearing to the Secretary of State to be suffering from a relevant disability or a prospective disability, be restricted so as to authorise only the driving of vehicles of a particular construction, or design specified in the licence, and...

3.9.3.1 Motor Bicycles and Mopeds

The Road Traffic Act 1988, s. 97 goes on to state that a provisional licence:

(3) ...

    (d) ...

    (e) except as provided under subsection (3B) below, shall not authorise a person, before he has passed a test of competence to drive, to drive on a road a motor bicycle or moped except where he has successfully completed an approved training course for motor cyclists or is undergoing training on such a course and is driving the motor bicycle or moped on the road as part of the training.

(3A) Regulations may make provision as respects the training in the driving of motor bicycles and mopeds of persons wishing to obtain licences authorising the driving of such motor bicycles and mopeds by means of courses of training provided in accordance with the regulations; and the regulations may in particular make provision with respect to—

    (a) the nature of the courses of training;

    (b) the approval by the Secretary of State of the persons providing the courses and the withdrawal of his approval;

    (c) the maximum amount of any charges payable by persons undergoing the training;

    (d) certificates evidencing the successful completion by persons of a course of training and the supply by the Secretary of State of the forms which are to be used for such certificates; and

    (e) the making, in connection with the supply of forms of certificates, of reasonable charges for the discharge of the functions of the Secretary of State under the regulations; and different provision may be made for training in different classes of motor bicycles and mopeds.

- propelled by electric power; or
- the cylinder capacity of its engine does not exceed 125 cc and the maximum net power output of its engine does not exceed 11 kW.

Unless drivers are exempted by the Regulations, they may not drive a motor bicycle or moped on a road before passing an approved training course or while on such a course as part of that training (s. 97(3)(e)). The regulation of approved training courses (also known as compulsory basic training—'CBT') for riders of motor bicycles is governed by part V of the 1999 Regulations. Among the other qualifications that such a person must have, an approved CBT instructor must show the Secretary of State that he/she is a 'fit and proper person'.

On completion of a CBT course a person will be issued with a certificate. This certificate will be valid for two years (reg. 68 as amended by the Motor Vehicles (Driving Licences) (Amendment) Regulations 2001 (SI 2001/53)).

As with other provisional licence holders, learner riders will be subject to the conditions set out in reg. 16. Regulation 16(7) requires such learners to:

- be in the presence and under the supervision of a certified direct access instructor
- be able to communicate with the instructor by means of a non hand-held radio system
- be wearing apparel (together with the instructor) which is fluorescent or, if during the hours of darkness, is either fluorescent or luminous.

An exception to the requirement for the learner to be in radio contact with the instructor has been inserted to cover the situation where the learner has a hearing impairment (reg. 16(11)). In such cases, it will suffice that the learner and the instructor employ a 'satisfactory means of communication' which they agree upon before the start of the journey.

The requirements that must be met by a 'direct access instructor' are set out under reg. 65. Note that, while conducting the above training, the maximum number of 'trainees' that a direct access instructor can supervise is two (reg. 67).

The requirement to have a qualified driver supervising the holder of a provisional licence on the vehicle does not apply when the licence holder is riding a moped, or motor bicycle with or without a sidecar (reg. 16(3)(b)).

Regulation 16(6) provides that the holder of a provisional licence authorising the driving of a moped, or motor bicycle with or without a sidecar, shall not drive such a vehicle while carrying another person. This creates an absolute ban on passengers, qualified or otherwise, on such vehicles being driven by provisional licence holders.

The Motor Vehicles (Driving Licences) (Amendment) Regulations 2001 impose additional requirements on holders of provisional licences to drive learner motor bicycles or mopeds. Regulation 16(7A) says that holders of a provisional licence for a learner motor bicycle or moped must not drive such a vehicle on a road when undergoing training (other than as part of an approved motor cyclists' training course) by a paid instructor unless the instructor is at all times present with them on the road and is supervising no more than three other such provisional licence holders.

3.9.3.2 Full Licences Used as Provisional

Section 98(2) of the Road Traffic Act 1988 provides that a person holding a full licence for certain classes of vehicle may drive motor vehicles of other classes as if authorised by a provisional licence for those other classes.

3.9.3.3 General Requirements for Provisional Licence Holders

Holders of a provisional licence must not drive or ride a motor vehicle of a class authorised by the licence unless under the supervision of a 'qualified driver' (reg. 16(2)(a) of the 1999 Regulations).

Regulation 17 defines a 'qualified driver':

(1) Subject to paragraphs (2) and (2A), a person is a qualified driver for the purposes of regulation 16 if he—

    (a) is 21 years of age or over,

    (b) holds a relevant licence,

    (c) has the relevant driving experience, and

    (d) in the case of a disabled driver, he is supervising a provisional licence holder who is driving a vehicle of a class included in Categories B, C, D, C + E, or D + E and would in an emergency be able to take control of the steering and braking functions of the vehicle . . .

(2A) For the purposes of supervising the holder of a provisional licence driving a vehicle of a class included in sub-category C1, C1+E, D1 or D1+E ('the learner vehicle') which the holder is authorised to drive by that licence, a person is not a qualified driver unless that person has, in addition to meeting the requirements specified in paragraph (1), passed a test in which the vehicle used in the practical test fell within the same sub-category as that of the learner vehicle.

KEYNOTE

A 'relevant licence' means a full licence (including a Northern Ireland or Community licence) authorising the driving of vehicles of the same class as the vehicle being driven by the provisional licence holder (reg. 17(3)(c)). In the case of disabled drivers it means a full licence authorising the driving of a class of vehicles in category B other than invalid carriages. The reference to para. (2) is to people who are members of the armed forces acting in the course of their duties. 'Relevant driving experience' is defined at reg. 17(3)(e). Generally people will have relevant driving experience if they have held the relevant full licence for a continuous or aggregate period of not less than three years including any period when they have held a provisional licence and a valid test pass certificate entitling them to a full licence for the driving of vehicles of the same class. Other conditions setting out 'relevant driving experience' are imposed by reg. 17(3) in relation to the supervision of people driving vehicles in categories C, D, C + E and D + E.

Specific provision is made for the supervision of learner drivers by drivers who are disabled.

Provisional licence holders must display the 'distinguishing mark' (L plate) in the form set out at part 1 of sch. 4 in such a manner that it is clearly visible to other persons using the road from within a reasonable distance from the front and back of the vehicle (reg. 16(2)(b)). Provisional licence holders driving a motor vehicle on a road in Wales may display the alternative distinguishing mark (a 'D' plate, signifying *dysgwr* or 'learner' (reg. 16(4)).

The requirement to have a qualified driver supervising them does not apply to vehicles in certain categories that are constructed or adapted to carry only one person (reg. 16(3)), neither does it apply to motor bicycles or mopeds.

Provisional licence holders are generally prohibited from drawing trailers although certain classes of vehicles are exempt from this provision (reg. 16(2)(c)).

If a person is disqualified until passing another test and then fails to abide by the provisions of the new provisional licence, he/she commits the offence of driving while disqualified (under s. 103 of the Road Traffic Act 1988).

If provisional licence holders fail to observe these conditions, they commit an offence under s. 91 of the Road Traffic Offenders Act 1988 (i.e. breaching the Regulations); if they do *not have* a provisional licence they commit the offence under s. 87 of driving otherwise than in accordance with a licence.

KEYNOTE

Regulation 80 makes provision for holders of foreign licences to be treated as holders of relevant driving licences under part III of the Road Traffic Act 1988 for certain purposes. These requirements only apply in relation to the requirements of s. 87(1) (driving otherwise than in accordance with a licence) and therefore do not entitle such licence holders to supervise learner drivers. Holders of such licences may, if they take out a provisional licence in the United Kingdom, not have to comply with the general requirements imposed on learner drivers (see para. 3.9.3).

3.9.4 | Supervision of Learner Drivers

There is only one acceptable minimum standard of driving and all drivers, *including learners*, must observe it; if not, they commit the offence of careless driving (*McCrone* v *Riding* [1938] 1 All ER 157).

A supervisor of a learner driver is not required to provide tuition to the learner, but to 'supervise'. That means doing whatever might reasonably be expected to prevent the learner driver from acting carelessly or endangering others (*Rubie* v *Faulkner* [1940] 1 All ER 285). The duty includes being in a position to take control of the vehicle in an emergency. If the supervisor is not able to do this, either because of his/her physical state (e.g. being drunk) or being out of the vehicle (e.g. giving directions), the condition will not have been fulfilled.

In the context of drink/drug driving offences, the role of the supervisor is particularly relevant, both to the offence and any available defences. In *DPP* v *Janman* [2004] EWHC 101 (Admin) it was held that, in any ordinary case, the person supervising a learner driver is in control of the vehicle and this was the obvious and normal consequence of that role. This factual state of affairs did not require proof that the supervisor was a 'qualified driver' under the regulations (see below). Therefore, if the supervisor's blood/alcohol level exceeded the prescribed limit or the concentration of specified controlled drug in blood/urine was above a specified limit, the supervisor would commit the offence under s. 5(1)(b) or s. 5A of the Road Traffic Act 1988 (in charge of a motor vehicle whilst over the prescribed limit) simply by supervising a learner driver on a road or in a public place. Additionally, the contingent role of the supervisor, i.e. having to be ready to take actual control of the vehicle at any point, means that it is almost impossible to argue the defence under s. 5(2) and s. 5A(6) of the Act because that defence requires defendants to show that there was no likelihood of their driving while still over the limit. The whole purpose of supervising a learner is to intervene as and when it becomes necessary and therefore there is *every likelihood* of the supervisor having to drive during the journey.

Whether or not a supervisor fulfilled his/her duty will be a question of fact for a court to determine in each case. If it can be shown that the qualified person was not actually 'supervising' the driver then the requirement under reg. 16 (**see para. 3.9.3.3**) will not have been observed and the offence (under s. 91 of the Road Traffic Offenders Act 1988) will be committed. That offence will be aided and abetted by the so-called supervisor.

A 'supervisor' can also be convicted of aiding and abetting where the learner driver is over the prescribed limit or unfit through drink or drugs (*Crampton* v *Fish* (1969) 113 SJ 1003).

The duties of a supervisor extend to ensuring compliance with other legislative requirements made of drivers such as remaining at the scene of an accident (*Bentley* v *Mullen* [1986] RTR 7).

OFFENCE: **Supervisor of Learner Driver Failing to Give Details—*Road Traffic Act 1988, s. 165(5)***
- Triable summarily • Fine

The Road Traffic Act 1988, s. 165 states:

(5) A person—
   (a) who supervises the holder of a provisional licence granted under Part III of this Act while the holder is driving on a road a motor vehicle (other than an invalid carriage), or
   (b) whom a constable or vehicle examiner has reasonable cause to believe was supervising the holder of such a licence while driving, at a time when an accident occurred owing to the presence of the vehicle on a road or at a time when an offence is suspected of having been committed by the holder of the provisional licence in relation to the use of the vehicle on a road,

   must, on being so required by a constable or vehicle examiner, give his name and address and the name and address of the owner of the vehicle.

3.9.5 Instruction of Learner Drivers

Anyone is able to give driving lessons provided they do not charge money or money's worth in return. Anyone who wants to give driving instruction for payment must be registered in accordance with the provisions of part V of the Road Traffic Act 1988 (s. 123). The purpose of the regulation of driving instructors was examined in *Mahmood* v *Vehicle Inspectorate* (1998) 18 WRTLB 1 where it was held that notions of contractual payment under civil law were not particularly helpful or relevant. What mattered was whether or not the defendant (instructor) had some sort of arrangement with the learner driver and that the arrangement had a 'commercial flavour'.

Police driving instructors are exempt from this requirement (s. 124) (this includes the proper giving of instruction in accordance with arrangements by the National Crime Agency).

Free driving lessons offered by someone in the business of buying and selling cars will be deemed to be given for payment if they are given in connection with the supply of a vehicle (s. 123(3)).

These restrictions only apply to 'motor cars' as specifically designed for this purpose, therefore it would not prevent someone charging for driving lessons on motor cycles or other vehicles falling outside the definition.

3.9.6 Driving Tests

Sections 89 and 89A of the Road Traffic Act 1988 impose the need to pass a prescribed driving test before being granted a licence, while part III of the Motor Vehicles (Driving Licences) Regulations 1999 (as amended) makes provisions for those driving tests along with the various exemptions from any part of the test that may apply. The content of the test itself includes a two-part theory test, with the second part covering hazard perception.

A person conducting a driving test must be satisfied as to the applicant's identity. The only document that is acceptable as proof of identity in this regard is a valid passport (except in relation to tests run by the armed forces) (reg. 38). Purporting to be someone else when taking a test will involve offences of fraudulently creating or using documents. Under regs 23 and 24, chief officers of police may conduct driving tests for their personnel under certain conditions.

3.9.6.1 Between Driving Test and Issue of Licence

Regulation 16(10) of the 1999 Regulations makes provision for the situation where provisional licence holders have been issued the relevant certificate stating that they have passed a driving test but have not yet received their full licence. In such cases, the requirements to display 'L' (or 'D') plates and to be supervised, together with the restrictions on the carrying of passengers, are removed.

3.9.7 | New Drivers

Once learner drivers have passed the prescribed test, there are further specific considerations with regard to their standard of driving in the first two years. The Road Traffic (New Drivers) Act 1995 places additional requirements on recently qualified drivers by setting out a probationary period during which time the accumulation of a reduced number of penalty points will result in their licence being revoked.

The Road Traffic (New Drivers) Act 1995 states:

1.—(1) For the purposes of this Act, a person's probationary period is, subject to section 7, the period of two years beginning with the day on which he becomes a qualified driver.

    (2) For the purposes of this Act, a person becomes a qualified driver on the first occasion on which he passes—

        (a) any test of competence to drive mentioned in paragraph (a) or (c) of section 89(1) of the Road Traffic Act 1988;

        (b) any test of competence to drive conducted under the law of

            (i) another EEA State,

            (ii) the Isle of Man,

            (iii) any of the Channel Islands, or

            (iv) Gibraltar.

    ...

2.—(1) Subsection (2) applies where—

        (a) a person is the holder of a licence;

        (b) he is convicted of an offence involving obligatory endorsement;

        (c) the penalty points to be taken into account under section 29 of the Road Traffic Offenders Act 1988 on that occasion number six or more;

        (d) the court makes an order falling within section 44(1)(b) of that Act in respect of the offence;

        (e) the person's licence shows the date on which he became a qualified driver, or that date has been shown by other evidence in the proceedings; and

        (f) it appears to the court, in the light of the order and the date so shown, that the offence was committed during the person's probationary period.

    (2) Where this subsection applies, the court must send to the Secretary of State—

        (a) ...

        (b) on their production to the court, the person's licence.

KEYNOTE

The above legislation sets out a probationary period of two years beginning when the driver passed a test of competence to drive either in the United Kingdom or in another European Economic Area country. If, during that time, the driver receives six or more penalty points on his/her licence, the full entitlement to drive will be lost and the driver will have to pass another test of competence in the category of vehicle which he/she was entitled to drive (s. 4). The Divisional Court has confirmed that, if drivers attract penalty points as a result of an offence committed while holding a *provisional* licence and then receive further points in the first two years of holding a full licence taking them to six or more points in all, the Secretary of State has no alternative but to revoke the licence under the provisions of s. 3 (*R (On the Application of Adebowale)* v *Bradford Crown Court* [2004] EWHC 1741 (Admin)).

3.9.8 | Classes and Categories of Vehicle Licensed

Section 87 of the Road Traffic Act 1988 requires that all those driving a motor vehicle on a road do so in accordance with a licence authorising them to drive a motor vehicle *of that class*.

The classification of vehicles is created by virtue of reg. 4 of the Motor Vehicles (Driving Licences) Regulations 1999 and sch. 2 to those Regulations. In relation to licences granted before 1 January 1997, provisions for the change from the 'old' categories to the new ones are to be found in reg. 76.

Regulation 7 of the 1999 Regulations sets out the categories of vehicle that a driver will be deemed as competent to drive by virtue of holding a licence. This regulation restricts drivers who passed tests in relation to certain restricted classes of vehicle (e.g. those with an automatic transmission) to vehicles falling within that category or sub-category. Similar provisions apply under reg. 7 to drivers having adaptations in relation to a disability. The categories of vehicle that a licence holder is entitled to drive will be clearly marked on their licence and any relevant restrictions will appear in the information codes in section 12.

3.9.9 Minimum Ages

The ages at which a person may drive the relevant category are generally to be found in the Road Traffic Act 1988, s. 101, although some of the restrictions on additional categories under reg. 7 also include references to minimum ages.

These amendments are *very detailed* and are frequently updated. Therefore reference should be made to the Regulations themselves wherever possible and again the DVLA is probably the best source of up-to-date information in this respect.

3.9.10 Driving Otherwise than in Accordance with Licence

The current categories of vehicles for the purposes of driving licences are to be found in sch. 2 to the 1999 Regulations.

OFFENCE: **Driving Otherwise than in Accordance with Licence—*Road Traffic Act 1988, s. 87***
> • Triable summarily • Fine • Discretionary disqualification for s. 87(1) under specified circumstances

The Road Traffic Act 1988, s. 87 states:

(1) It is an offence for a person to drive on a road a motor vehicle of any class otherwise than in accordance with a licence authorising him to drive a motor vehicle of that class.

(2) It is an offence for a person to cause or permit another person to drive on a road a motor vehicle of any class otherwise than in accordance with a licence authorising that other person to drive a motor vehicle of that class.

KEYNOTE

Where a defendant is charged with driving otherwise than in accordance with a licence and driving without insurance, once the prosecution have proved that the defendant has driven on a public highway, it is for the defendant to show that he/she had a driver's licence and insurance as those matters were within the defendant's knowledge. In addition, there is no obligation on the police to serve any request for production of the relevant documentation (*DPP* v *Hay* [2005] EWHC 1395 (Admin)).

This offence will apply where a person has a particular licence and has failed to abide by any conditions attached to it, or where a person does not hold a licence at all. In proving such an offence, you must show that the defendant drove a motor vehicle on a road; it is then for the defendant to show that he/she had a licence to do so (*John* v *Humphreys* [1955] 1 WLR 325).

Section 88 provides a long list of exceptions to the general prohibition imposed by s. 87. Those exemptions include:

• Drivers who have had their licence revoked on disqualification and who have re-applied for another.
• Drivers who have a 'qualifying application' lodged with the Secretary of State.
• Drivers from overseas becoming resident in Great Britain.

3.9.11 | Disqualification from Driving

Most disqualifications are imposed by the courts under part II of the Road Traffic Offenders Act 1988. Some special provisions exist in relation to the disqualification of holders of large goods or passenger-carrying vehicles licences (see the Road Traffic Act 1988 s. 115 and the Driving Licences (Community Driving Licence) Regulations 1998 (SI 1998/1420)). Many drivers also find themselves disqualified by reason of the 'totting up' procedure whereby, once you have accumulated 12 penalty points within three years of the commission of the first offence, you are subject to a mandatory minimum period of six months' disqualification. In addition, s. 146 of the Powers of Criminal Courts (Sentencing) Act 2000 makes provision for courts to disqualify defendants convicted of any offence, instead of or as well as any other punishment. Note that where an offender is disqualified penalty points in respect of that offence must not additionally be endorsed (*R* v *Usaceva* [2015] EWCA Crim 166). The court can disqualify even if the defendants are passengers and not drivers. An attempt was made by four men to break into a cash machine. A police pursuit began when the men drove off at high speed. Speeds of up to 150 mph were recorded in the pursuit. Two passengers were disqualified (as was the driver) until an extended driving test was passed. The Court of Appeal held that it was right to order disqualification until an extended driving test was taken, even as passengers (*R* v *Beech and others* [2016] EWCA Crim 1746).

Similarly, where a court convicts a person of common assault or of any other offence involving an assault (including an offence of aiding, abetting, counselling or procuring, or inciting), that person can be disqualified if the assault was committed by driving a motor vehicle. In the case of the Crown Court, if it is satisfied that a motor vehicle was used *by the person convicted or by anyone else* for the purpose of committing, or facilitating the commission of, the offence in question, the court may order the person convicted to be disqualified (s. 147). Facilitating the commission of an offence includes the taking of any steps after the offence has been committed for the purpose of disposing of any property to which it relates or of avoiding apprehension or detection (s. 147(6)).

Where a court sentences an individual to an immediate custodial sentence as well as ordering the individual to be disqualified for holding or obtaining a licence, the court must add an extension period to the disqualification period to take into account the time spent in custody (s. 137 of the Coroners and Justice Act 2009).

3.9.11.1 | Special Reasons Not to Disqualify

Section 34(1) of the Road Traffic Offenders Act 1988 outlines that where a person is convicted of an offence involving obligatory disqualification the court must order him to be disqualified for such period not less than 12 months as the court thinks fit unless the court for special reasons thinks fit to order him to be disqualified for a shorter period, or not to order him to be disqualified. In *DPP* v *Bristow* [1998] RTR 100 the Divisional Court stated that the key question justices should ask themselves when assessing if such special reasons existed on which they might decide not to disqualify was this: what would a sober, reasonable and responsible friend of the defendant, present at the time, but himself a non-driver and thus unable to help, have advised in the circumstances, to drive or not to drive? This is an 'objective' test which was affirmed in *Key* v *CPS* [2013] EWHC 245 (Admin). This 'objective' test was examined by the appeal court in Scotland in relation to a police officer who had pleaded guilty to a s. 2 of the Road Traffic Act 1988 offence whilst driving to an 'urgent assistance' call and disqualified despite asserting special reasons not to, i.e. the circumstances of the call. The appeal court found the sheriff in the original case focused more on 'neutral issues', like the officer was not an accredited emergency driver, rather than the circumstances and having considered those they quashed the disqualification (*Natasha Watt against Procurator Fiscal, Aberdeen* [2016] SAC (Crim) 16 SAC/2016/000169/AP).

OFFENCE: **Driving while Disqualified—*Road Traffic Act 1988, s. 103(1)(b)***

> • Triable summarily • Six months' imprisonment and/or a fine • Discretionary disqualification

The Road Traffic Act 1988, s. 103 states:

> (1) A person is guilty of an offence if, while disqualified for holding or obtaining a licence, he—
> (a) ...
> (b) drives a motor vehicle on a road.

OFFENCE: **Obtaining Licence while Disqualified—*Road Traffic Act 1988, s. 103(1)(a)***

> • Triable summarily • Fine

The Road Traffic Act 1988, s. 103 states:

> (1) A person is guilty of an offence if, while disqualified for holding or obtaining a licence, he—
> (a) obtains a licence...

KEYNOTE

A licence obtained by a person who is disqualified is of no effect (s. 103(2)).

In *Shackleton* v *Chief Constable of Lancashire Police* [2001] EWCA Civ 1975, the Court of Appeal set out the key issues to be considered when looking at an offence of driving while disqualified. In that case the defendant was known to be a disqualified driver and was seen by a police officer to be 'jogging' away from a parked Ford Escort. The officer followed and arrested him under the former statutory power. In hearing the defendant's appeal against the lawfulness of his arrest, the court said that the primary issue was whether the defendant had driven the car or whether the police officer had the reasonable belief that he had driven it. Guidance on this issue was to be found in *Pinner* v *Everett* [1969] 1 WLR 1266 where the House of Lords concluded that each case had to be considered on its merits. Their lordships had also held that there was no requirement for the vehicle to be in motion and that the key considerations in assessing each case on its merits were whether the defendant:

- had actually stopped driving or intended to carry on driving (e.g. at a set of traffic lights)
- was still driving
- had arrived at his/her destination or intended to continue to a further location
- had been prevented or persuaded from driving by someone else.

If the person is disqualified *by reason of age* (under s. 101), this offence will not apply; the relevant offence would be under s. 87(1).

The offence of driving while disqualified is one of strict liability and there is no need to show that the driver knew of the disqualification (*Taylor* v *Kenyon* [1952] 2 All ER 726).

You must prove that the person who was driving the motor vehicle was in fact disqualified. This may sound obvious but it has occasionally been overlooked, causing problems at trial (*R* v *Derwentside Magistrates' Court, ex parte Heaviside* [1996] RTR 384). Although one way of proving that a defendant was disqualified at the time of driving is by a certificate under s. 73(4) of the Police and Criminal Evidence Act 1984, this is by no means the only way of so proving. The courts have accepted the evidence of someone who was present in court at the time the person was disqualified (*Derwentside*); they have also accepted the defendant's own admission that he was disqualified, both in interview under caution and in evidence before the court (*Moran* v *CPS* (2000) 164 JP 562 and *DPP* v *Mooney* [1997] RTR 434).

A person may still commit the offence(s) above even if the disqualification is later quashed on appeal; the offence is complete as long as the person was disqualified at the relevant time (*R* v *Lynn* [1971] RTR 369).

As the offence of driving while disqualified is a summary offence, it cannot be 'attempted'.

If a passenger genuinely believes that the driver is entitled to drive the vehicle in which they are both found, that belief will prevent the passenger being charged with 'aiding and abetting' the offence under s. 103(1)(b) (*Bateman* v *Evans* (1964) 108 SJ 522). In the case of someone supervising a 'learner driver' who turns out to be disqualified, it seems reasonable to expect a supervisor to establish that the driver under his/her supervision has a current and valid licence before venturing out onto the road.

| **Disqualification until Test is Passed**

The Road Traffic Offenders Act 1988, s. 36 states:

(1) Where this subsection applies to a person the court must order him to be disqualified until he passes the appropriate driving test.
(2) Subsection (1) above applies to a person who is disqualified under section 34 of this Act on conviction of—
   (a) manslaughter, or in Scotland culpable homicide, by the driver of a motor vehicle, or
   (b) an offence under section 1 (causing death by dangerous driving), section 1A (causing serious injury by dangerous driving) or section 2 (dangerous driving) of the Road Traffic Act 1988.
(3) Subsection (1) above also applies—
   (a) to a person who is disqualified under section 34 or 35 of this Act in such circumstances or for such period as the Secretary of State may by order prescribe, or
   (b) to such other persons convicted of such offences involving obligatory endorsement as may be so prescribed.
(4) Where a person to whom subsection (1) above does not apply is convicted of an offence involving obligatory endorsement, the court may order him to be disqualified until he passes the appropriate driving test (whether or not he has previously passed any test).
(5) In this section—
   'appropriate driving test' means—
   (a) an extended driving test, where a person is convicted of an offence involving obligatory disqualification or is disqualified under section 35 of this Act,
   (b) a test of competence to drive, other than an extended driving test, in any other case,
   'extended driving test' means a test of competence to drive prescribed for the purposes of this section, and 'test of competence to drive' means a test prescribed by virtue of section 89(3) of the Road Traffic Act 1988.

KEYNOTE

Section 36 gives the court the power to disqualify a person from holding or obtaining a licence (s. 98(1)) until the person passes an 'appropriate' test. If the person is disqualified under the provisions for 'totting up' penalty points (s. 35) or is found guilty of an offence involving obligatory disqualification (s. 34), the 'appropriate' test is an extended test as defined at s. 36(5)(b). In other cases the 'appropriate' test will be a regular driving test under s. 89(3) of the Road Traffic Act 1988.

Section 36(3)(b) enables the Secretary of State to add further offences to the list. This has been done in relation to an offence under s. 3A of the Road Traffic Act 1988 (causing death by careless driving when under the influence of drink or drugs). In the case of an offence under s. 3A the relevant test is an extended driving test.

Where a person is convicted of an offence involving obligatory disqualification that is not covered by s. 36(1) and (2) (e.g. an offence under s. 4(1) of the Road Traffic Act 1988), the court may order disqualification until that person passes an appropriate driving test (s. 36(4)). Here the appropriate test will generally be the regular driving test (unless the disqualification involves 'totting up'). In determining whether or not to disqualify a person in such a case, the court must have regard to the safety of road users (s. 36(6)).

Section 36(7)–(13) make provision for the extent and effect of a disqualification until a test is passed and also provide for tests of competence in certain other European countries to be treated as meeting the requirements of s. 36.

A person disqualified from holding a licence until he/she has passed another driving test is a disqualified person for the purposes of s. 103. Such persons are forbidden to drive unless they can bring themselves within the provisions of the Act with regard to provisional licences. In effect, they are given a limited right to drive, as an exception, notwithstanding the fact that they have been disqualified (*Scott* v *Jelf* [1974] RTR 256). One effect of this is that where a person so disqualified obtains a provisional licence and then drives without supervision or 'L' plates, he/she commits an offence of driving while disqualified under s. 103 (*Scott* v *Jelf*). In addition, this also means that the burden of proving that the exception applies rests with the driver (partly as a result of s. 101 of the Magistrates' Courts Act 1980). The effect of this is that it will fall to the driver to show that, not only did he/she have a provisional licence at the time, but that he/she was driving in accordance with the conditions of that licence. The absence of any such evidence means that, once it is proved that a defendant

---

was the driver of a vehicle at a particular time, the court should have convicted him/her of the offence of driving while disqualified (*DPP* v *Barker* [2004] EWHC 2502 (Admin)).

A person who has been disqualified until he/she has passed a test can apply for a provisional licence and can drive in accordance with the conditions of such a licence (s. 37(3)). After all, it is the purpose of such a disqualification that offenders be required to prove their competence to drive, rather than simply removing them from the road.

The courts have a power to impose an interim disqualification under certain conditions. Where a defendant has been convicted of a relevant offence under ss. 34 to 36 and the magistrates' court commits the defendant to the Crown Court *for sentence*, the court may order an interim disqualification (see s. 26(1) of the Road Traffic Offenders Act 1988 and s. 6 of the Powers of Criminal Court (Sentencing) Act 2000). The magistrates' court may also impose an interim disqualification when:

- remitting the person to another magistrates' court (under s. 10 of the Powers of Criminal Court (Sentencing) Act 2000);
- deferring passing a sentence on the person; or
- adjourning after convicting the person but before dealing with him/her for the offence.

A magistrates' court cannot impose an interim disqualification when committing a defendant *for trial*.

3.9.11.3 After Disqualification has Expired

- Once a period of disqualification ends, the person may apply for another licence.
- On application for another licence the person falls within the category of someone who 'has held and is entitled to obtain' a licence under s. 88 of the Road Traffic Act 1988.
- Section 88 provides an exemption to the offence of driving otherwise than in accordance with a licence (s. 87).
- The person can begin to drive again as soon as a proper application has been received by the Driver and Vehicle Licensing Agency.

If a person drives before applying for a new licence he/she commits the offence under s. 87.

A person disqualified until passing a driving test may (or, in order ever to drive again, *must*) apply for a provisional licence. On application the person may begin to drive in accordance with the conditions below.

A person who receives a disqualification period of less than 56 days (called a Short Period Disqualification) will have his driving record updated by the court with details of the disqualification. The licence will become valid again the day after the expiry of the disqualification and the person can then drive again without the need to apply to the DVLA for return of the licence (see s. 37(1A) of the Road Traffic Offenders Act 1988).

KEYNOTE

Section 88 of the Road Traffic Act 1988 sets out exceptions to the general requirement for anyone wishing to drive a motor vehicle on a road to have an appropriate driving licence.

High Risk Offenders (who have been disqualified by court order as a result of serious drink-driving related offences, as prescribed under s. 94(4) of the 1998 Act by reg. 74(1) of the Motor Vehicles (Driving Licences) Regulations 1999) who are in the process of applying for a driving licence as a result of, or in anticipation of, the expiry of a driving disqualification, are prevented from driving before they have successfully been granted a new licence following a medical examination as required by the Secretary of State (under s. 94(5) of the Act). This only applies where the conviction in respect of which the disqualification was imposed is on or after the section was brought into force (1 June 2013).

Driving while Disqualified in Another Country

Disqualification from holding or obtaining a licence in one country does not necessarily prevent the person from driving in another country. However a number of initiatives have been put in place to deal with these situations. A person who is disqualified by a court in Northern Ireland from holding or obtaining a Northern Ireland licence will also be disqualified from holding or obtaining a driving licence issued by the DVLA (s. 102A of the Road Traffic Act 1988).

3.9.12 Drivers from Other Countries

The entitlement of drivers living outside the United Kingdom to drive here under the authority of their overseas permits is governed by the Motor Vehicles (International Circulation) Order 1975 (SI 1975/1208). If such drivers hold a domestic or Convention driving permit issued abroad or a British Forces driving licence, they may drive the vehicles covered by those authorities in Great Britain for one year (Article 2). Regulation 80 of the Motor Vehicles (Driving Licences) Regulations 1999 makes similar provisions in relation to people who become resident in the United Kingdom. That permit allows holders to take a driving test in that 12-month period. If they do not do so successfully then they will need a GB provisional licence.

Visitors and new residents holding a valid driving licence may also use that licence during the first 12 months and, if they apply for a GB provisional licence during that period, they will be exempt from the conditions imposed on provisional licence holders (reg. 18).

Members of visiting forces and their dependants are covered by the Motor Vehicles (International Circulation) Order 1975, as amended (Article 3).

The law governing drivers from EU Member States can now be found in the Driving Licences (Community Driving Licence) Regulations 1996 (SI 1996/1974).

Drivers from EU Member States must meet the fitness requirements of British drivers and, provided they are not disqualified, drivers meeting those physical requirements may exchange their licence for a part III licence if they have become normally resident in Great Britain (s. 89 of the Road Traffic Act 1988).

The 1988 Act also makes provision for the exchange of other licences from some non-EU countries.

Section 97(1) of the Road Traffic Act 1988 has been modified by the Motor Vehicles (Driving Licence) (Amendment) Regulations 2012 to prevent drivers disqualified in a European Economic Area State where they formerly held a licence from being granted a licence in Great Britain (including a provisional licence).

The Driving Licences (Exchangeable Licences) (Amendment) Order 2013 (SI 2013/22) designates countries and territories for the purpose of allowing driving licences issued in them to be exchanged for a driving licence issued in Great Britain.

3.9.13 Physical Fitness and Disability

The Road Traffic Act 1988, s. 92 states:

(1) An application for the grant of a licence must include a declaration by the applicant, in such form as the Secretary of State may require, stating whether he is suffering or has at any time (or, if a period is prescribed for the purposes of this subsection, has during that period) suffered from any relevant disability or any prospective disability.

(2) In this Part of this Act—
    'disability' includes disease and the persistent misuse of drugs or alcohol, whether or not such misuse amounts to dependency,
    'relevant disability' in relation to any person means—
    (a) any prescribed disability, and

(b) any other disability likely to cause the driving of a vehicle by him in pursuance of a licence to be a source of danger to the public, and

'prospective disability' in relation to any person means any other disability which—

(a) at the time of the application for the grant of a licence or, as the case may be, the material time for the purposes of the provision in which the expression is used, is not of such a kind that it is a relevant disability, but

(b) by virtue of the intermittent or progressive nature of the disability or otherwise, may become a relevant disability in course of time.

(3) If it appears from the applicant's declaration, or if on inquiry the Secretary of State is satisfied from other information, that the applicant is suffering from a relevant disability, the Secretary of State must, subject to the following provisions of this section, refuse to grant the licence.

KEYNOTE

If driving licences have been refused or revoked on medical grounds (including eyesight), the Secretary of State may serve a notice (under s. 94(5)(c) of the Road Traffic Act 1988) requiring applicants to take a specific driving test in order to assess their fitness—a 'disability assessment test'. In such cases the person may be granted a disability assessment licence which is an authority to drive only *for the purposes of taking such a test*.

The 1999 Regulations make special provision for drivers who suffer from epilepsy who may obtain a Group 1 licence as long as they have been free from an attack over the preceding 12 months or have only suffered from those attacks while asleep.

A person refused a licence may appeal against that decision under s. 100.

A court has a duty to notify the Secretary of State if it appears that a person has a relevant disease or disability (s. 22 of the Road Traffic Offenders Act 1988).

The Secretary of State may attach conditions to a licence in light of any disability of the holder. If holders do not observe those conditions, they commit the offence under s. 87(1).

Section 94 (see below) imposes a requirement for licence holders to notify the Secretary of State *in writing*, of any relevant disability which has either not been disclosed in the past or which has become more acute since the licence was granted.

The 1999 Regulations set out the conditions under which the Secretary of State may require (under s. 94) applicants for a licence to undergo a medical examination if they have convictions for drink/driving offences.

3.9.13.1 | **Notification of Disability**

OFFENCE: **Failing to Give Notification of Relevant Disability—*Road Traffic Act 1988, s. 94(3)***

- Triable summarily • Fine

The Road Traffic Act 1988, s. 94 states:

A person who fails without reasonable excuse to notify the Secretary of State as required by subsection (1) above is guilty of an offence.

OFFENCE: **Driving Motor Vehicle before Giving Notification of Disability—*Road Traffic Act 1988, s. 94(3A)***

- Triable summarily • Fine • Discretionary disqualification

The Road Traffic Act 1988, s. 94 states:

(3A) A person who holds a licence authorising him to drive a motor vehicle of any class and who drives a motor vehicle of that class on a road is guilty of an offence if at any earlier time while the licence was in force he was required by subsection (1) above to notify the Secretary of State but has failed without reasonable excuse to do so.

3.9.13.2 | Driving after Refusal or Revocation of Licence

OFFENCE: **Driving Motor Vehicle after Refusal or Revocation—*Road Traffic Act 1988, s. 94A***

> • Triable summarily • Six months' imprisonment and/or a fine • Discretionary disqualification

The Road Traffic Act 1988, s. 94A states:

(1) A person who drives a motor vehicle of any class on a road otherwise than in accordance with a licence authorising him to drive a motor vehicle of that class is guilty of an offence if—
  (a) at any earlier time the Secretary of State—
    (i) has in accordance with section 92(3) of this Act refused to grant such a licence,
    (ii) has under section 93 of this Act revoked such a licence, or
    (iii) has served notice on that person in pursuance of section 99C(1) or (2) or 109B of this Act requiring him to deliver to the Secretary of State a Community licence or Northern Ireland licence authorising him to drive a motor vehicle of that or a corresponding class, and
  (b) since that earlier time he has not been granted—
    (i) a licence under this Part of this Act, or
    (ii) a Community licence or Northern Ireland licence,
  authorising him to drive a motor vehicle of that or a corresponding class.

3.9.13.3 | Driving with Uncorrected Defective Eyesight

OFFENCE: **Driving with Uncorrected Defective Eyesight—*Road Traffic Act 1988, s. 96(1)***

> • Triable summarily • Fine

The Road Traffic Act 1988, s. 96 states:

> If a person drives a motor vehicle on a road while his eyesight is such (whether through a defect which cannot be or one which is not for the time being sufficiently corrected) that he cannot comply with any requirement as to eyesight prescribed under this Part of this Act for the purposes of tests of competence to drive, he is guilty of an offence.

KEYNOTE

Under s. 96(2) a constable having reason to suspect that a person driving a motor vehicle may be guilty of this offence may require that person to submit to an eyesight test. Refusing to do so is a further offence under s. 96(3).

The specific requirements as to eyesight are:

- characters 79 mm high and 57 mm wide
- on a registration mark
- fixed to a motor vehicle
- at 20.5 metres
- in good light (with the aid of corrective lenses if worn at the time).

However, the regulations take into account the changes to the dimensions of vehicle registration plate characters and, if the narrower characters (50 mm wide) are used, the relevant distance for the above test is generally 20 metres (this is a lesser requirement than that imposed on applicants taking driving tests, where the relevant distance is generally 27 metres). For this reason it would seem that an eyesight test under s. 96(2) ought to be carried out under the same conditions, though there is no direct authority on the point.

One source of a police officer's 'reasonable suspicion' under s. 96(2) might be the information code on the driver's photocard licence which will state whether the holder has any eyesight correction.

The police are able to take immediate action against motorists who fail roadside eye tests. The system enables the police to notify the DVLA electronically with details of eyesight test failures allowing a notice of revocation of the licence to be issued to motorists within hours. Previously, the police notified the DVLA in writing or by fax which in some cases meant that the revocation could take up to four days. Motorists who commit the offence under s. 96(1) will have their licence revoked. The licence will not be returned until drivers can demonstrate that their eyesight meets the required standard. The police will be able to contact the DVLA between 8 am and 9 pm. Roadside eyesight tests can only be carried out in daylight. On evenings and weekends, where the police deem the circumstances merit immediate action, they can use their powers to impose bail conditions. These can include requiring the person not to drive as a condition of bail. If a person subject to a 'no-drive' condition broke it, he/she could be taken to court to reconsider the question of bail.

Inability to read the characters as set out in the regulations will amount to a prescribed disability for the purposes of s. 92(2) (see para. 3.9.13).

3.9.14 The Road Traffic (Driver Licensing and Information Systems) Act 1989

The purpose of this Act is to provide a unified information system about and for drivers, under the authority of the Secretary of State.

Part I of the 1989 Act introduces a unified licensing system, providing for the licensing of drivers and setting out the requirements of drivers, including their suitability to hold the relevant licence.

The Act provides the Secretary of State with powers to refuse driving licences to some applicants or to revoke existing licences on grounds of physical unfitness.

Part II of the Act provides for the introduction of driver information systems which will collect, store, process and transmit data on 'driver information'. Such systems are intended to help drivers in relation to traffic routes, congestion, etc. The systems are to be provided by operators licensed to do so by the Secretary of State. Operating an unlicensed system is an offence (s. 9).

3.9.14.1 Access to Driver Licensing Records

Under s. 71(2) of the Criminal Justice and Court Services Act 2000, the Secretary of State may make available any information held (e.g. by the DVLA) under part III of the Road Traffic Act 1988 to the police and the National Crime Agency. When making this information available, the Secretary of State may determine the *purposes* for which constables may be given that information and also the *circumstances* under which constables may further disclose the information they have been given.

In the Motor Vehicles (Access to Driver Licensing Records) Regulations 2001 (SI 2001/3343), the Secretary of State has set out both the purposes for which the information may be given to police officers and the circumstances under which officers can further disclose it.

Under reg. 2 of the 2001 Regulations, the purposes are the prevention, investigation or prosecution of a contravention of any provision under the following:

- the Road Traffic Act 1988
- the Road Traffic Offenders Act 1988

and also for ascertaining whether persons have had an order made in relation to them under the various statutes that allow for their disqualification from driving (namely the Child Support Act 1991, s. 40B and the Criminal Justice Act 2003, s. 301(2)).

Under reg. 3, the circumstances under which officers may further disclose the information that they have been given are:

- where the information is passed to an employee of a police authority, local policing body or chief officer of police
- for any purpose ancillary to, or connected with, the use of the information by the officers.

A new system of endorsing driving licences enables the Secretary of State to make arrangements for the access to information held on a person's 'driving record' as held at the DVLA, irrespective of whether or not that person holds a driving licence. The driving record will contain particulars of any endorsements. This is particularly relevant when dealing with an offence under the fixed penalty procedure when it is important to be able to ascertain if people have existing penalty points which, when added to the penalty points available for the offence under consideration, would make them liable to disqualification under the 'totting up procedure'. The Road Traffic Offenders Act 1988 provides:

97A Meaning of 'driving record'

(1) In this Act 'driving record', in relation to a person, means a record in relation to the person maintained by the Secretary of State and designed to be endorsed with particulars relating to offences committed by the person under the Traffic Acts.

(2) The Secretary of State may make arrangements for the following persons to have access, by such means as the Secretary of State may determine, to information held on a person's driving record—

(a) courts,

(b) constables,

(c) fixed penalty clerks,

(d) the person in respect of whom the record is maintained and persons authorised by him, and

(e) other persons prescribed in regulations made by the Secretary of State.

(3) The power to make regulations under subsection (2)(e) above shall be exercisable by statutory instrument.

(4) No regulations shall be made under subsection (2)(e) above unless a draft of the instrument containing them has been laid before, and approved by a resolution of, each House of Parliament.

3.10 Notices of Intended Prosecution

This chapter is only tested in the Sergeants' examination—Inspectors' examination candidates should not study this material.

3.10.1 | Introduction

Section 1 of the Road Traffic Offenders Act 1988 outlines that before certain offences can be prosecuted:

- the defendant must have been warned of the possibility of that prosecution at the time of the offence (s. 1(1)(a)); or
- the defendant must have been served with a summons (or charged) within 14 days of the offence (s. 1(1)(b)); or
- a notice setting out the possibility of that prosecution must have been sent to the driver or registered keeper of the vehicle within 14 days of the offence (s. 1(1)(c)).

The notice or warning must be given by the 'prosecutor' which will ordinarily be the police. If the person giving it is not empowered to make a decision whether or not to prosecute (such as a vehicle examiner employed by the vehicle inspectorate), the warning or notice will not be deemed to have been served (*Swan* v *Vehicle Inspectorate* [1997] RTR 187).

The notice referred to is a Notice of Intended Prosecution (NIP). If a verbal warning is given at the time it must be shown that the defendant understood it (*Gibson* v *Dalton* [1980] RTR 410). Proof that the defendant understood it will lie on the prosecution and, for that reason, it is common practice to send a NIP whether a verbal warning was given or not.

3.10.2 | Relevant Offences

The offences which require a NIP are listed in sch. 1 to the Road Traffic Offenders Act 1988 and include:

- Dangerous, careless or inconsiderate driving.
- Dangerous, careless or inconsiderate cycling.
- Failing to comply with traffic signs and directions.
- Leaving a vehicle in a dangerous position.
- Speeding offences under ss. 16 and 17 of the Road Traffic Regulation Act 1984.

The list of offences in sch. 1 is exhaustive; other offences, even if similar in nature to those in the list, will not be covered by the requirements of s. 1(1) (*Sulston* v *Hammond* [1970] 1 WLR 1164).

3.10.3 | Exceptions

Section 2(1) of the Road Traffic Offenders Act 1988 states that the requirement to serve a NIP does not apply in relation to an offence if:

- at the time or
- immediately afterwards and

- owing to the presence of the vehicle concerned
- on a road
- an accident occurred.

Each of these features must be present to remove the need for a NIP to be served or a warning given.

'Accident' is broader than the expression used under s. 170 of the Road Traffic Act 1988. However, although such 'reportable' accidents extend to public places as well as roads, the exemption under s. 2(1) is limited to an accident that occurs on *a road* at the time or immediately after the offence.

Whether the accident occurred 'at the time' is a matter of fact and degree (*R* v *Okike* [1978] RTR 489).

If the driver is unaware that the accident has taken place because it is so minor, there *will* be a need to serve a NIP (*Bentley* v *Dickinson* [1983] RTR 356). The thinking behind this ruling is that the warning or NIP will allow the driver to gather evidence to answer any charge arising from the accident.

Where the accident is so severe that the driver has no recollection of it, there is no need to serve a NIP and the ruling in *Bentley* will not apply (*DPP* v *Pidhajeckyj* [1991] RTR 136).

There must be some causal connection between the presence of the vehicle concerned and the accident (*Quelch* v *Phipps* [1955] 2 QB 107).

Section 2 goes on to say:

(2) The requirement of section 1(1) of this Act does not apply in relation to an offence in respect of which—
  (a) a fixed penalty notice (within the meaning of Part III of this Act) has been given or fixed under any provision of that Part, or
  (b) a notice has been given under section 54(4) of this Act.
(3) Failure to comply with the requirement of section 1(1) of this Act is not a bar to the conviction of the accused in a case where the court is satisfied—
  (a) that neither the name and address of the accused nor the name and address of the registered keeper, if any, could with reasonable diligence have been ascertained in time for a summons or, as the case may be, a complaint to be served or for a notice to be served or sent in compliance with the requirement, or
  (b) that the accused by his own conduct contributed to the failure.

KEYNOTE

Failure to observe the requirements of s. 1(1) will not bar an alternative conviction which is allowed under s. 24, that is, where the original offence was not one requiring a NIP but where the alternative offence *would* ordinarily require such a notice (s. 2(4)).

If the defendant contributes to the failure to serve the NIP, then that failure will not be a bar to conviction.

3.10.4 | **Proof**

The Road Traffic Offenders Act 1988, s. 1 states:

(1A) A notice required by this section to be served on any person may be served on that person—
  (a) by delivering it to him;
  (b) by addressing it to him and leaving it at his last known address; or
  (c) by sending it by registered post, recorded delivery service or first class post addressed to him at his last known address.
(2) A notice shall be deemed for the purposes of subsection (1)(c) above to have been served on a person if it was sent by registered post or recorded delivery service addressed to him at his last known address, notwithstanding that the notice was returned as undelivered or was for any other reason not received by him.
(3) The requirement of subsection (1) above shall in every case be deemed to have been complied with unless and until the contrary is proved.

KEYNOTE

As discussed at **para. 3.10.1**, the warning may be oral (under s. 1(1)(a)) but there are problems of proof where such warnings are given. If the defendant was preoccupied at the time or can show that he/she did not fully understand what was being said, the provisions of s. 1(1) will not have been complied with.

Serving a NIP personally on the spouse or partner of the defendant would appear to be enough (*Hosier* v *Goodall* [1962] 2 QB 401).

If the defendant is not at his/her home address, for instance because he/she is in hospital or on holiday, service to the defendant's last known address will suffice even if the police are aware of that fact (*Phipps* v *McCormick* [1972] Crim LR 540).

If neither the defendant nor the registered keeper has any fixed abode, reasonable efforts must be made to serve the notice personally. If such efforts fail, s. 2(3) would apply and the need for service would be removed.

Although any of the methods of posting set out at s. 1(1A)(c) will suffice, if the question of posting is challenged, evidence of posting may be required. There is an irrebuttable presumption that if a NIP is sent by registered post or recorded delivery then it has been served within two days. However it is a rebuttable presumption if the notice is sent by first class post if the defence can give evidence that the notice was received after the 14-day period (*Gidden* v *Chief Constable of Humberside* [2009] EWHC 2924 (Admin)).

As the purpose of the warning or notice is to alert the defendant to the likelihood of prosecution, it is not necessary to specify exactly which offence is being considered; it is enough that the defendant is made aware of the *nature* of the offence (*Pope* v *Clarke* [1953] 1 WLR 1060).

Section 1(3) places the burden of proving non-conformity with the requirement on the defence.

3.11 Forgery and Falsification of Documents

> This chapter is only tested in the Sergeants' examination—Inspectors' examination candidates should not study this material.

3.11.1 | Introduction

Much of the law regulating road policing depends on the production and examination of documents. This chapter deals with occasions where a suspect has, or uses, false documentation. When dealing with such occasions, it is important to consider the overlapping legislation which deals with forgery and fraud generally.

3.11.2 | The Offences

Road traffic law is heavily reliant on forms and documents. Therefore it is important that any documents are genuine and reliable. Many further road traffic offences involve the fraudulent creation and use of documents, some of which are summarised below.

3.11.2.1 | Forgery of Documents

OFFENCE: **Forgery of Documents—*Road Traffic Act 1988, s. 173***
  - Triable either way • Two years' imprisonment and/or a fine on indictment
  - Fine summarily

The Road Traffic Act 1988, s. 173 states:

(1) A person who, with intent to deceive—
  (a) forges, alters or uses a document or other thing to which this section applies, or
  (b) lends to, or allows to be used by, any other person a document or other thing to which this section applies, or
  (c) makes or has in his possession any document or other thing so closely resembling a document or other thing to which this section applies as to be calculated to deceive,
  is guilty of an offence.

KEYNOTE

'Forges' for this purpose means making a false document or other thing in order that it may be used as genuine (s. 173(3)).

In each of the circumstances set out in s. 173(1)(a)–(c) you must show an intention to deceive, making this a crime of 'specific intent'.

The documents to which these offences apply are set out in s. 173(2) and include:

- licences
- test certificates

- certificates of insurance
- certificates exempting the wearing of seat belts
- any document evidencing the successful completion of a driver training course provided in accordance with regulations under s. 99ZA of the Act.

'Calculated to deceive' (s. 173(1)(c)) means likely to deceive. Where a defendant produces a certificate of insurance issued under a policy which has since been cancelled, this offence may be made out (*R* v *Cleghorn* [1938] 3 All ER 398).

3.11.2.2

False Statements or Withholding Information

OFFENCE: **False Statements and Withholding Information—*Road Traffic Act 1988, s. 174***

- Triable either way • Two years' imprisonment on indictment
- Six months' imprisonment and/or fine summarily

The Road Traffic Act 1988, s. 174 states:

(1) A person who knowingly makes a false statement for the purpose—
  (a) of obtaining the grant of a licence under any Part of this Act to himself or any other person, or
  (b) of preventing the grant of any such licence, or
  (c) of procuring the imposition of a condition or limitation in relation to any such licence, or
  (ca) of obtaining a document evidencing the successful completion of a driver training course provided in accordance with regulations under section 99ZA of this Act, or
  (d) of securing the entry or retention of the name of any person in the register of approved instructors maintained under Part V of this Act, or
  (dd) of obtaining the grant to any person of a certificate under section 133A of this Act, or
  (e) of obtaining the grant of an international road haulage permit to himself or any other person,
  is guilty of an offence.

(2) A person who, in supplying information or producing documents for the purposes either of sections 53 to 60 and 63 of this Act or of regulations made under sections 49 to 51, 61, 62 and 66(3) of this Act—
  (a) makes a statement which he knows to be false in a material particular or recklessly makes a statement which is false in a material particular, or
  (b) produces, provides, sends or otherwise makes use of a document which he knows to be false in a material particular or recklessly produces, provides, sends or otherwise makes use of a document which is false in a material particular,
  is guilty of an offence.

(3) A person who—
  (a) knowingly produces false evidence for the purposes of regulations under section 66(1) of this Act, or
  (b) knowingly makes a false statement in a declaration required to be made by the regulations,
  is guilty of an offence.

(4) A person who—
  (a) wilfully makes a false entry in any record required to be made or kept by regulations under section 74 of this Act, or
  (b) with intent to deceive, makes use of any such entry which he knows to be false,
  is guilty of an offence.

(5) A person who makes a false statement or withholds any material information for the purpose of obtaining the issue—
  (a) of a certificate of insurance or certificate of security under Part VI of this Act, or
  (b) of any document issued under regulations made by the Secretary of State in pursuance of his power under section 165(2)(a) of this Act to prescribe evidence which may be produced in lieu of a certificate of insurance or a certificate of security,
  is guilty of an offence.

3.11.2.3 Issuing False Documents

OFFENCE: **Issue of False Documents—*Road Traffic Act 1988, s. 175***

  • Triable summarily • Fine

The Road Traffic Act 1988, s. 175 states:

If a person issues—
  (a) any such document as is referred to in section 174(5)(a) or (b) of this Act, or
  (b) a test certificate or certificate of conformity (within the meaning of Part II of this Act),
and the document or certificate so issued is to his knowledge false in a material particular, he is guilty of an offence.

3.11.2.4 Police Powers

The Road Traffic Act 1988, s. 176 states:

(1) If a constable has reasonable cause to believe that a document produced to him—
  (a) in pursuance of section 137 of this Act, or
  (b) in pursuance of any of the preceding provisions of this Part of this Act,
  is a document in relation to which an offence has been committed under section 173, 174 or 175 of this Act or under section 115 of the Road Traffic Regulation Act 1984, he may seize the document.
(1A) ...
(2) When a document is seized under subsection (1) above, the person from whom it was taken shall, unless—
  (a) the document has been previously returned to him, or
  (b) he has been previously charged with an offence under any of those sections,
  be summoned before a magistrates' court . . . to account for his possession of the document.
(3) ...
(4) If a constable, an examiner appointed under section 66A of this Act has reasonable cause to believe that a document or plate carried on a motor vehicle or by the driver of the vehicle is a document or plate to which this subsection applies, he may seize it.
  For the purposes of this subsection the power to seize includes power to detach from a vehicle.
(5) Subsection (4) above applies to a document or plate in relation to which an offence has been committed under sections 173, 174 or 175 of this Act in so far as they apply—
  (a) to documents evidencing the appointment of examiners under section 66A of this Act, or
  (b) to goods vehicle test certificates, plating certificates, certificates of conformity or Minister's approval certificates (within the meaning of Part II of this Act), or

    (c) to plates containing plated particulars (within the meaning of that Part) or containing other particulars required to be marked on goods vehicles by sections 54 to 58 of this Act or regulations made under them, or

    (d) to records required to be kept by virtue of section 74 of this Act, or

    (e) to international road haulage permits.

(6) When a document or plate is seized under subsection (4) above, either the driver or owner of the vehicle shall, if the document or plate is still detained and neither of them has previously been charged with an offence in relation to the document or plate under section 173, 174 or 175 of this Act, be summoned before a magistrates' court . . . to account for his possession of, or the presence on the vehicle of, the document or plate.

KEYNOTE

This extensive power also allows (where appropriate) for the items to be detached from the vehicle (s. 176(4)). The power under subs. (4) is restricted to officers who are authorised vehicle examiners.

The references in s. 137(1) of the Act and s. 115 of the Road Traffic Regulation Act 1984 relate to the registration of driving instructors and the misuse of parking documents respectively.

Index